LESS IS MORE

A PRACTICAL GUIDE TO WEEDING SCHOOL LIBRARY COLLECTIONS

DONNA J. BAUMBACH AND LINDA L. MILLER

University of Central Florida
Florida SUNLINK Project

AMERICAN LIBRARY ASSOCIATION
Chicago   2006

While extensive effort has gone into ensuring the reliability of information appearing in this book, the publisher makes no warranty, express or implied, on the accuracy or reliability of the information, and does not assume and hereby disclaims any liability to any person for any loss or damage caused by errors or omissions in this publication.

The paper used in this publication meets the minimum requirements of American National Standard for Information Sciences—Permanence of Paper for Printed Library Materials, ANSI Z39.48-1992. ∞

Library of Congress Cataloging-in-Publication Data

Baumbach, Donna J. (Donna Jean), 1948-
    Less is more : a practical guide to weeding school library collections /
Donna J. Baumbach & Linda L. Miller.
        p.   cm.
    Includes index.
    ISBN 0-8389-0919-1
    1. Discarding of books, periodicals, etc. 2. School libraries—Collection development. I. Miller, Linda L., 1943- . II. Title.
    Z703.6.B38 2006
    025.2'16—dc22   2006007490

Printed in the United States of America

10   09   08   5   4   3   2

To family and friends who supported us as we took time away from them to put this book together

To the thousands of library media specialists on LM_NET who have used the SUNLINK Weed of the Month and provided feedback on its usefulness

To the SUNLINK staff who graciously added Weed of the Month to the growing list of "labors of love" because it was the right thing to do for Florida school library media programs and Florida students

To students everywhere—in the hope that they will always have school library media centers that are inviting and up to date; that they will *want* to visit the library media center; that they *will* always find something "good to read"; and that they will value and know how to use the information they find

CONTENTS

FOREWORD

SUNLINK—Florida's K–12 union database project—began with funding appropriations passed during the 1988 and 1989 legislative sessions. High school librarians across the state hurriedly began reading about *MA*chine *R*eadable *C*ataloging (MARC) and retrospective conversion. Collection assessments followed as library media specialists readied their libraries for the SUNLINK application. The first group of schools to be admitted to the project received their acceptance news in the spring of 1990.

Important criteria in the application process involved verifying that the collection had been weeded and that the shelflist was accurate and up to date. On the application, the library media specialist also noted the last date weeding activity occurred and the number of items discarded. Through the years, the number of discards reported varied widely from zero to over seven thousand items per school.

Emphasizing the maintenance aspect of collection development has always been an important component of the SUNLINK project. Initial SUNLINK membership included retrospective conversion of the shelflist to MARC format, involving a variable cost per record. Deleting items from the collection and shelflist before the conversion is, therefore, cost effective. However, just as important is maintaining the accuracy of the union database. Library media specialists are obligated to maintain accurate records of additions, deletions, and changes in catalog records each year. This responsibility reflects the need for a continuous and sustainable weeding program.

Weed of the Month was the SUNLINK project's answer to assisting library media specialists with this responsibility. Weed of the Month provided guidelines for a manageable and, therefore, sustainable collection maintenance program. It offered a weeding-by-class approach that breaks down the overwhelming collection maintenance responsibility into manageable monthly chunks. It narrowed the work scope and made the process practical for the busy school librarian. Additionally, Weed of the Month gave justifications for the discards, which could be communicated to the administration, if necessary.

Initially, SUNLINK's Weed of the Month idea and specific suggestions originated from LM_NET, an electronic discussion list for librarians.

Eventually, the Weed of the Month program became nationally recognized among school library media specialists as a reputable source for weeding as well as purchasing suggestions. Today, links to this resource are commonly found on state, district, and school Internet sites around the country.

SUNLINK's program not only created more knowledgeable library media specialists; administrators and teachers are now more aware of the evaluative criteria needed for different areas of the collection. Through Weed of the Month, they have developed a respect for the knowledge needed to maintain a "healthy" collection.

During the early years of the project, SUNLINK was distributed on a CD-ROM, and each school's collection was accessible only by other participating schools. However, when the Internet-delivered version was introduced, visibility of each school's collection—strengths and weaknesses— became worldwide.

SUNLINK's Weed of the Month program proved to be an invaluable tool for librarians across the country in maintaining the integrity of quality collections. Today more than ever, maintaining a current collection and providing quality, accurate information is vital to the long-term success of school library media programs. I am pleased to see the weeding criteria updated for this book, gathered in one place, and surrounded by other helpful information about weeding for busy school library media specialists.

Nancy L. Teger, Sc.D.
Program Specialist
Library Media Services
Florida Department of Education

For more than a dozen years, LM_NET has defined itself as a virtual home to school librarians worldwide, via the unique contributions made by its members. The SUNLINK Weed of the Month Club, with LM_NET for more than half our existence, has been one of the most valuable and regular contributions to our online community. We appreciate the fact that SUN-LINK has chosen LM_NET as its venue to introduce a new weeding subject area each month since September 1997.

Like many others, I was saddened to learn that the Club would be ceasing its monthly postings to LM_NET. However, in the fine tradition of giving and sharing, all was not to be lost. The Weed of the Month Club will continue to be available in print form, and thus readily available to those who are unable to go online. Our LM_NET members will dearly miss the Weed of the Month Club, but fortunately, its helpful guidelines are now printed here in this handy volume.

Peter Milbury
LM_NET Co-Founder and Moderator

PREFACE

SUNLINK is Florida's K–12 public school online union catalog of library media holdings. Begun in 1988, it is a huge library automation project funded annually by the Florida legislature to increase Florida students' access to information.

Just as schools struggle to do the most with the little money they have, so does the SUNLINK project. Early in the automation game it became apparent that for both logical and financial reasons, schools need to weed ruthlessly before undergoing retrospective conversion. Why spend money to put something in the database that shouldn't be on the shelves, only to pay to remove it later?

Thus began our mission: to get schools to weed their collections—but not just for automation or for the project. Weed because it is the right thing to do for your students!

On May 4, 1997, Dr. Mike Eisenberg posted this message to LM_NET:

> You know what really bugs me? Hearing about library collections that have books on the shelves about the space program or astronomy that were written before we put a man on the moon! How many times have we heard this? I say enough!! Here's what I suggest/request: let's start a worldwide movement: the "global let's get rid of outdated space/astronomy books challenge."

This was followed by much discussion on LM_NET of weeding and the sadly out-of-date space and astronomy titles people found on their shelves. LM_NETer Karen DeFrank of Glassboro, New Jersey, suggested that LM_NET have a targeted weed of the month—a topic that would be explored for weeding criteria. The SUNLINK staff loved the idea and decided not only to adopt it for use with our Florida schools but to share our efforts with LM_NET where the idea began. Every month of the school year since fall 1997, the SUNLINK Weed of the Month has been published on the World Wide Web and announced on LM_NET. LM_NETers continued to suggest topics for weeding, helped develop criteria in areas of their own expertise, added titles that should be weeded, and identified titles for replacing the weeded items.

We knew we had a hit on our hands when we were barraged by e-mails if the Weed of the Month topic was not posted to the Web on the first of the month—even if that date fell on a weekend! Using search engines to see who links to SUNLINK's Weed of the Month, we have been surprised and delighted to see that it has become part of district library media program websites and one of public librarians' favorite links, and is frequently mentioned by library schools in class syllabi.

Looking back over Weed of the Month topics, we found that even weeding criteria began to need weeding after eight years, and revising and updating led us to wonder if gathering all the topics in one volume and adding some practical words of wisdom would be of value to anyone. That remains to be seen, of course, but now you know how this book evolved. And we believe that this work will be of considerable value to all school library media specialists facing the daunting and often overwhelming task of weeding.

Yogi Berra said, "In theory there is no difference between theory and practice. In practice, there is." We have undertaken every effort to make this book practical. The tone is intended to be light and conversational. We've included some of our favorite quotations about weeding—including some that might be stretched to imply they are about weeding—that we've encountered along the way in our careers. We've tried to use a little humor from time to time to keep it interesting to you and to us, but our real hopes are that this book helps school library media specialists answer the questions of why and how to weed, that it motivates busy professionals to get weeding despite the size or age of the collection, and that as a result, K–12 school library media collections will improve, attracting more students to come to the library media center to use and value the wealth of accurate, up-to-date information provided for them.

How is this book organized? Chapter 1 includes a general rationale for weeding school library media collections and many of the excuses for not weeding that we've encountered along the way. You'll see that we believe there is no excuse for not weeding. Chapter 2 describes general weeding guidelines and offers helpful hints for those about to undertake a weeding project of any size, and chapter 3 describes where to start (Anywhere! Just start!) and provides some information about how the weeding topics in chapter 4 are organized. Chapter 4 is really the heart of the book, and it includes seventy-one weeding topics, some new to Weed of the Month and many updated and revised. Chapter 5 describes general ways to use library automation systems in weeding and collection development, and chapter 6 talks about what to do—and what not to do—with the items you've weeded as well as the general housekeeping required to keep your records as accurate and up to date as your collection. We've provided a list of some World Wide Web sites that offer more information—both theory and practice—about weeding, and we've included notes about weeding different areas of the collection by Dewey number with the topics covered in chapter 4 identified.

We certainly must acknowledge the contributions of the SUNLINK staff to the SUNLINK Weed of the Month. Carol McWilliams fielded e-mail from around the world about the topics and faithfully posted the topic of the month to LM_NET during the school year. Matt Renfroe and Kathy Katz designed the Weed of the Month web pages and kept them up to date and accessible on the SUNLINK server. John Prevosk reviewed the topics each month and included weeding in his training around the state. Debbie Culp, our office manager, kept us all on the straight and narrow, ensuring a pleasant environment in which to develop the Weed of the Month and other "far-out" ideas of the SUNLINK staff. She and a variety of student assistants over the years have organized monthly mailings to all Florida schools, including the Weed of the Month topics.

Special thanks to Sandy Ulm, mother of SUNLINK—now retired from the Florida Department of Education—for her vision and her understanding that building a state database of library media holdings must encompass more than gathering, merging, and deduping records; to Nancy Teger, current library media program specialist at the DOE, for continued support, for encouraging us to develop this work, and for moving all of us in new directions; to FAME and lobbyists Mary Margaret Rogers and Bob Cerra for keeping the funding for SUNLINK coming; and to the folks at Brodart Automation for indulging our every whim. Thanks, too, to Susan Veccia who told us we could write this book and then gently guided us through the process!

Chapter One

The Role of Weeding in Collection Development (Why Less Is More)

PICTURE THIS

It seemed like a simple assignment: "Write a report on one country in Africa." The list of things to include in the report would be easy to find. And elementary school friends Allison and Caroline knew just where to get the information they needed: their school library media center. It always had the information they needed. They didn't even need to use the online catalog for this one. Allison went right to the 900s, geography and history, and scanned the shelves. There, right next to one another, were two books on an African country she didn't know anything about: The Belgian Congo. Caroline scanned the shelves and selected two books on Uganda. She didn't know about that country either, but her books were right next to Allison's choices, so she thought that was a perfect choice for a best friend to make!

Allison and Caroline both checked out their books, read them carefully, and created their multimedia reports. The reports were beautiful! They included everything the teacher required: population, type of government, leaders, major religions, flag, economy, neighboring countries, housing. The girls each had an "A" project for sure.

Caroline did get an A indeed! She had learned a lot about Uganda and its people. But when Allison got the grade on her report, she was shocked to see an F! Population: wrong! Type of government: wrong! Leaders: wrong! Economy: wrong! Flag: wrong! How could this be? She had checked and cited both sources carefully. She got the information from the books in the library media center! Her teacher must be wrong!

No, Allison. Sorry. Both books you used had publication dates in the 1950s. The Belgian Congo became an independent nation in 1960 and much has changed, including the name of the country. The books Caroline used were published recently. Both girls worked side by side and put the same amount of effort in their reports. The age of the resources made all the difference in the reports and, more importantly, in what was learned.

* * *

Far-fetched? Not really. We teach our students they can rely on the library media center for information, but unfortunately, many school library media centers have some pretty old stuff on the shelves. The books Allison used have been around more than four times as long as she has been alive!

You might argue that as part of information literacy, we teach students to look at publication dates, and Allison should have known that she was using old information. Perhaps that is true. Certainly, looking at copyright and publication dates is integral to judging the credibility of sources, a skill we want to develop. But should those books be on the shelf in the first place now that we are well into the twenty-first century? Absolutely not.

Although this scenario may be a bit extreme, we hope it will cause you to think about your own collection. Do you have items on your shelves that are dated in the 1960s or 1970s (or earlier) and have titles that include the words "Now" or "Today"? Walk the shelves with us a bit. Do these books give themselves away by virtue of the words in their titles?

America My Home, Then and Now, 1937

America Votes: Things You Should Know
about Elections Today, 1976

American Sports Heroes of Today, 1970

The Arab World Today, 1960

The Face of Cuba Today, 1961

Flying Saucers, Here and Now, 1967

Now in Mexico, 1947

Patterns of Ethics in America Today, 1960

Russians, Then and Now, 1961

These are real examples we found through school library media centers' online catalogs. Just by looking at the titles, you can see why these books might be appealing to young people. By adding the publication dates, however, you can probably see that the books really need to be discarded.

Do some of your books on space travel talk about sending a man to the moon in the future? Do any of your materials on the stock market indicate that it is always a sound investment? Do some of your materials on diabetes, cancer, AIDS, and other diseases reflect the progress that has been made in recent decades? Do most of your materials on the Civil War look as though they were published at the time of the conflict? Do you have any materials whose titles reflect our "forty-eight states"? Although students should keep the publication date in mind as they read a book or know to use more current materials, many of them are not able to sort this out, and they simply end up getting bad information.

Age and lack of accurate information are not the only reasons to weed. Are some of your books in pitiful physical condition? Are some of them covered with mold and mildew? With crayon or marker stains? With peanut butter and jelly? Do you have multiple copies of things that are seldom used? Do you have materials that have not circulated in years and years? Do you have some AV (audiovisual) formats that are obsolete? Do you have books with reading levels too advanced for your students that might get more use at a higher grade level?

It does not matter how many books you may have, but whether they are good or not.

—Lucius Annaeus Seneca

Library media materials need to be reviewed and weeded regularly. Along with selection and purchasing, weeding is a critical part of developing and maintaining a balanced, relevant collection. Library media centers are not archives. They must be sources of current, dynamic, curriculum-related information for today's students.

When students first realize that information is what they need, we want them to think of the library media center and its resources. If we want students to use the information we are providing, we must be sure it is accurate and relevant, or they may go elsewhere.

WHAT IS WEEDING AND WHY SHOULD I DO IT?

Simply put, weeding is selection in reverse. It is deselection. Weeding is the act of reevaluating items in the collection and removing any that are inaccurate, out of date, misleading, inappropriate, unused, in poor condition, or otherwise harmful to students. It is something all librarians and library media specialists must do regularly if they want to maintain the best possible collections for their school communities. It is a professional responsibility that cannot be taken lightly.

We're not sure how "weeding" became the word for the process, although it is very similar to what is required in maintaining a beautiful, healthy garden. If you don't pull the weeds in a garden, they will overtake the flowers and vegetables you've planted, and even the most robust of plants won't survive.

If you don't weed a school library media center, students can get dangerous or misleading information. At best, they will learn not to trust the information they find in the media center. At worst, they could be hurt. Much of what we know now about health and nutrition will not be found in materials from thirty or forty years ago; in fact, most that was written then has turned out to be wrong. Not too long ago, we believed there were only nine planets; recently a possible tenth has been discovered. Some of our heroes have turned out to be bad guys. Older materials have words, images, and ideas that may reflect sexism, ageism, or racism. We've received "gift books" we would never have purchased because of their poor quality or factual errors.

In this age of rapidly changing information, it is imperative that we keep our collections up to date. This means selecting and purchasing new materials and discarding or recycling others.

Weeding has many benefits. As you weed, you will get to know the collection better and you will be better able to get the right "stuff" into the right hands at the right time. You may find great resources that would be used if promoted or if you sent them to a different school with a higher or lower grade level. You may find books that just need a new cover in order to be as inviting and attractive as you know they are. You may find "holes" in the collection—areas where you need to concentrate some funding to obtain resources to meet curricular and recreational needs. You may find items that have been assigned the wrong classification number or that may be better used if shelved under a different topic.

Once you weed thoroughly, you'll find your shelves and your library media center look better. You will have more space. The collection will be more appealing to teachers and students, although they may not even know why. They will notice that resources look more attractive and are easier to access. The "good stuff" will be more apparent to your users and not hidden among the dusty, dull volumes. Most importantly, students will find what they need to do their assignments and answer their questions honestly and accurately.

The bottom line: Why should you weed? Because your students deserve the best collection you can offer them. Less is more. Discard the items that need to go and you'll have more space, more "curb appeal," and more accurate, more relevant, more appropriate resources. The shelves in your library media center should reflect the ability of the collection to meet the teaching and learning needs of your school community.

EXCUSES, EXCUSES (AND WHY THEY DON'T HOLD WATER)

We wish we could tell you that weeding is fun. Storytelling is fun. Opening boxes of new books is fun. Collaborating with creative teachers is fun. Weeding is not fun in comparison. But that doesn't mean it can be ignored, as has been the case in many schools. We've found that library school curriculum focuses on selection, cataloging, and utilization, but weeding basics may not be emphasized. Internships and field experiences are so chock-full of learning that the topic of weeding may not even come up. Your first years as a media specialist find you so busy that it is easy to not do something—like weeding—especially when you are getting to know the students, the teachers, the community, the collection, and the job, all at the same time.

We've heard many excuses for not weeding, but there really is no excuse. The most common excuses—and our answers to those excuses—include the following.

I'm proud to have such a large selection of materials for my students and teachers. It's the largest in the _____ [district, region, state, country, universe, solar system—we've heard them all]. Now repeat after us: "Quality, not quantity. Quality, not quantity. Quality, not quantity."

The library media specialist who was here before me never weeded. That's not an excuse. In fact, it may be one of the best reasons to begin to weed immediately. Weeding is an ongoing task, and if it hasn't been done in some time, it is going to be a big job! The longer you put it off, the more difficult it will become. There will be more obsolete materials, more damage, and a lot more work. (And when *you* change schools, you really don't want to be known as "the library media specialist who never weeded"!) We do suggest you wait one year to give yourself time to know the collection and your school community, and then do thorough weeding. More about that later.

I hate to throw things away. Some library media specialists are packrats. Others just love everything in the library media center—especially the things they have selected—and don't want to let anything go. Weeding doesn't always mean discarding. It could mean recycling items, distributing them to classrooms or teachers, or sending them to another school. (However, remember if the item is "too old" for your collection, it is also too old for classroom collections or other schools.) Once you begin weeding, you'll begin to see the benefits, and you'll want to keep going. It is important to remember that quantity does not guarantee quality.

As soon as I discard it, someone will ask for it. This could happen, but if the item hasn't been used in a while or shouldn't be used because of misleading information, it is highly unlikely that someone will suddenly want it. If anyone asks, you probably have other—and better—sources of the same information: a newer book, a website, a new CD-ROM. Most people are after specific information, not a specific item. Remember, there's always interlibrary loan.

We need all these materials to meet the accreditation standards. Although most accrediting agencies may require minimum quantities in library media materials, they generally specify "usable materials." Obsolete formats, items in raggedy condition, and out-of-date materials are not usable. Accrediting agencies are there to ensure that schools are meeting acceptable standards and providing quality instruction, facilities, and materials. The advent of online databases, audiovisual materials, blogs, RSS feeds, podcasts, websites, and wide area networks has made counting the items in your collection very difficult. Poor-quality materials of any kind should never be counted. Living in denial is not a good thing.

If I pulled everything from the shelf that needed to go, I wouldn't have anything left. Although we doubt that is the case, if your collection has not been weeded in some time and little purchasing has been done, you may be correct. You can't weed everything at once, however. You may need to weed some areas of the collection that are badly out of shape several different times over several years, becoming more and more critical with each pass through the shelves. Start with obvious weeds. You'll get a better idea of what you have and what needs to be weeded next. Always remember that misleading, inaccurate, out-of-date information is *never* better than no information. You want quality materials that meet the informational and recreational needs of students. If you truly are left with bare or almost bare shelves after a thorough weeding, this will send a clear message that you care about the information that students can access. It will also show that you need an adequate budget to maintain an adequate collection. Giving the illusion that you have a quality collection because the shelves are full is just that, an illusion. You will fool some of the people, but the ones who really count—your students and teachers—will see the truth.

My principal won't let me weed. Principals are professionals. They have specific roles and responsibilities. They have training and experience in many areas, but administration of the school library media center is generally not included in their education. Your principal will learn from you, and this may be some of the most important teaching you do.

You are a professional. You have specific roles and responsibilities. You have training and experience in collection development, and we hope that includes weeding. Talk with your principal. Share your collection development policy with him or her. Explain the rationale for weeding. Finally, show some examples of materials that need to be weeded and explain why.

Our teachers would think we were wasting resources. This is a great opportunity to work with your teachers. Just as you involve them in acquiring new materials to fit the curriculum, they can assist in weeding. They know the curriculum and their own content areas. Science teachers can easily spot outdated concepts and ideas. Social studies teachers understand the changing geopolitical world and want materials that reflect current and historical events accurately. Teachers of math, English, foreign languages, art, music, physical education, and vocational education as well as guidance counselors—all teachers—understand that things change rapidly, that curriculum changes, and that old materials do not contribute to a good learning environment. Enlist their support as you weed sections of the library media center.

Parents would think we are wasting taxpayer dollars. Parents usually get upset when they see dumpsters full of "good books" outside the school, and they deserve to be uncomfortable about that. But if you establish an ongoing weeding schedule, weeding a bit at a time, you probably won't have to fill any dumpsters. In any case, if a deep weeding is called for—and even if it isn't—taking a short time at a PTA meeting to explain how you select materials and how and why you deselect them is a good idea. Be sure you save a few good examples that will help parents understand weeding. These examples can be quite entertaining! Look at some of your older materials on careers or dating for some fun examples.

I don't know enough about some of the subject areas to weed them. No one knows everything, but anyone can learn. Do some reading on the subject area you're about to tackle. Examine current textbooks and professional publications. Go online. Talk to subject area teachers. Find a colleague with expertise and confidence in the subject and work together.

I simply don't have time. You don't have time to be sure students have physical and intellectual access to quality materials? That's the heart of your job! In the long run, weeding will save you time. There will be fewer materials to inventory, fewer materials to shelve, less handling of old materials, and fewer materials to search, and you'll have a better knowledge of the collection. Weeding doesn't have to be done all at one time or once a year. Taking a close look at small sections at a time will result in less frustration and better decisions.

> *One might liken a gardener, weeding his flowerbeds, to weeding the mind so only healthy thoughts grow.*
>
> —Joan Adams Burchell

We don't have the funds to replace the items that should be weeded. Not everything that is pulled from the shelves will need to be replaced. You may have other materials on the subject to provide adequate coverage. If you are discarding a book, think about online resources that might be available to provide the information. Create web pages with links to good, relevant resources. If a newer edition is available to replace a well-used volume, budget for it. Consider trading duplicate titles with another school in your district. Check with the public library to see what is available and steer students there. Remember, no information is better than wrong information.

I might make a mistake and throw away something I shouldn't. Everyone makes mistakes. Library media specialists are human. Establishing good criteria for weeding can help prevent mistakes. We have selection policies and procedures approved by our boards of education. We must also have deselection policies and procedures.

I might throw away a valuable work of literature. Few old books are worth very much. Even those "first editions" have little value after they have been used by hundreds of students and marred with your library ownership stamp, tape, barcodes, and other official library information. If you think, however, that you do have a rare book with great value, check it out online with a reputable source such as Powell's, AddALL, or Alibris (http://www .powells.com, http://www.addall.com, or http://www.alibris.com). Even eBay auctions and stores can give you an idea of whether it is worth $2,500 or $2.50, and for the most part, we're betting on the latter. Or take it to an antique book dealer you trust. You might indeed be surprised.

My collection is brand new, so it doesn't need weeding. We're guessing that as hard as you worked to select this new collection, you may have purchased a few mistakes—items that weren't quite as described, don't fit the curriculum, have inappropriate reading levels, or just don't belong in your collection. Weed them now.

Weeding will show that I've made mistakes in purchasing. Well, who hasn't? That doesn't mean the mistake should remain in the collection. On the other hand, if material is being weeded because it is falling apart from use, you know you made an excellent choice. If it hasn't been used, perhaps the curriculum has changed. As time passes, some things will become outdated. That's life. Get on with it!

I don't know where to begin. You can begin just about anywhere. If you're doing a massive weeding, you might want to follow the Dewey numbers from 000 through the 900s and then look at the fiction, reference, and AV sections. If the curriculum in one area is changing, begin there. Or begin with an area in which you have an interest and some expertise. The important part is to start and then to continue.

I don't know how to weed. Then this book is meant for you. We'll give you a rationale and specific criteria for many topics in your school library media center, and you can weed as much or as little as you desire (or as much or as little as your collection needs). We believe in taking it in small chunks so that it won't be overwhelming for you or your staff or your school community.

Top 10 Reasons to Weed

Checklist for juvenile nonfiction books that can be disposed of (with apologies to Letterman's Top 10 Lists):

10. If any part of the text says that "someday man may go to space."
9. If an illustration of a computer takes more than one page because of the size of the machine.
8. If the encyclopedia entry says, "This year's Grammy winners, The Beatles."
7. If it mentions the Soviet Union in the present or future tense.
6. If the book has no Dewey Decimal number because it predates Dewey.
5. If the word Microsoft refers to something small and not hard.
4. If the book was written before you were born because, really, nothing important happened before you.
3. If the book refers to New York as New Amsterdam.
2. If the book is about American history and you cannot find any mention of World War II.

And the number 1 reason to get rid of a Juvenile Nonfiction book:

1. If a history book only has two people listed: Adam and Eve.

—From Steve Smith, a nonlibrarian, to his librarian girlfriend

---

General Weeding Guidelines

- Policies and Procedures
- Time-Tested Models
- General Criteria for Weeding
- Items Not to Weed
- Helpful Hints

The Milk in the Refrigerator

The milk in the refrigerator is past the sell date, has an odor, and is curdled and lumpy. Would you:

- Keep it, because you don't know when you could get to the store to buy more? *Then why would you keep a book on the shelf with misinformation because you don' t know when you could replace it?*
- Keep it, because otherwise your refrigerator would look empty? *Then why would you keep outdated books on the shelf to preserve a fake collection size?*
- Give it to a neighbor to keep in his or her refrigerator? *Then why would you send outdated encyclopedias or other materials to a teacher for classroom use?*
- Donate it to a food pantry for hungry children? *Then why would you send outdated resources to be used by children in this or other countries?*

—Gail Dickinson in "Crying Over Spilled Milk"

POLICIES AND PROCEDURES

Most school districts and some states have written policies and approved procedures that govern both collection development and weeding. Before you begin to weed, be sure to check whether any written policies or procedure documents exist. If they do, read them and follow them to the letter. A carefully developed policy can not only guide your work but also alleviate some misunderstandings among those in your school community about the process.

If you don't have a written weeding policy, you might want to advocate for its development. This is best done at the district level, but if you need to develop your own, there are plenty of good models on the Internet to get you started.

Written policies and procedures should address all aspects of weeding. The following questions should be clearly answered:

> Who weeds the collection?
>
> What is the purpose of weeding?
>
> What criteria are applied?
>
> What professional tools are used in evaluating the collection and its materials?
>
> How regularly is weeding to take place?
>
> What is done with material removed from the collection?
>
> What are the step-by-step procedures to be followed in weeding?

TIME-TESTED MODELS

Probably the best-known name in the area of weeding is Stanley Slote, whose book *Weeding Library Collections: Library Weeding Methods* (Englewood, CO: Libraries Unlimited, 1997) is now in its fourth edition. Slote advocates that objective data such as the length of time an item is on the shelf between uses should be the primary consideration for weeding, theorizing that past use is the best predictor of future use.

Although use and circulation are important in making weeding decisions, "shelf time" is only one factor to consider. With newer technologies such as CD-ROMs and online databases available, print materials such as books may get less use, but those print resources are still important. Books may be useful for finding in-depth information and establishing context, for helping students who have difficulty reading from the computer screen, or for ensuring access to resources for those who are without computer access at home. On the other hand, the future evolves rapidly, making some items that have received a great deal of use in the past obsolete almost overnight. For many items, "past use" should remain just that: past. For example, a flurry of books was published in 1997 about Internet search engines. Google opened its doors in 1998. New search engines are being developed practically every minute, and features, strengths,

Poorly weeded collections are not the sign of poor budgets, but of poor librarianship. Period.

—Doug Johnson, "Weed!"
http://www.doug-johnson
.com/dougwri/weed.html

and weaknesses of each change constantly! So although those search engine books may have gotten a great deal of use in 1997 and 1998, they were almost irrelevant by 2000 and are worthless now.

Many have advocated finding better criteria than shelf time, and that generally means a more subjective approach. Much of the criteria used in weeding today's school library media centers are subjective, but then selecting materials is also subjective—whether selecting for purchase, selecting for a specific teacher's unit, or selecting for an individual student's needs. We can't really fathom weeding based solely on numeric data; it is a professional task relying on professional knowledge and skills.

Nevertheless, we give Stanley Slote his props. Few have written with such passion and detail about weeding and its advantages to the collection and the user. He helped us all to understand that libraries—and especially school library media centers—must not be archives but modern, changing sources of current and relevant information.

CREW. One of the most widely recognized models for weeding is the CREW method. CREW is an acronym for Continuous Review, Evaluation, and Weeding. CREW is designed for small and medium-sized public libraries, but with a little tweaking, it can be used by school library media centers as well. The CREW method was developed by Joseph Segal and further refined and updated by Belinda Boon in *The CREW Method: Expanded Guidelines for Collection Evaluation and Weeding for Small and Medium-Sized Public Libraries.* It is available online as web pages (html) or in Adobe Acrobat (pdf) format from http://www.tsl.state.tx.us/ld/pubs/crew/index.html, or, if you prefer a bound copy, it is available for nominal cost from the Texas State Library.

CREW considers both objective and subjective criteria in the evaluation process. In the CREW method, there are two primary objective factors to consider: the age of the material, and circulation or use. Numbers in a formula indicate these objective criteria. For various Dewey classifications, the CREW manual provides guidelines for both age and use, indicated this way: 10/3/MUSTIE. In this formula, the 10 indicates the material should be discarded if the last publication date was over ten years ago. The 3 indicates the item should be discarded if more than three years have passed since it has circulated. MUSTIE refers to more subjective criteria that we'll describe later in this chapter. Some selections are described as X/X/MUSTIE, or 5/X/MUSTIE. An X in either position indicates that age or use or both do not need to be considered for that topic.

These objective guidelines can be adjusted for specific needs. For example, if the formula is 8/3/MUSTIE and your shelves are very crowded, you might decide to change the formula to 5/3 or even 5/2. On the other hand, if this is the first weeding in a long time, you will probably want to be more conservative and change the formula to 10/3 or 10/4. That way, less will be eliminated on these objective criteria alone.

There are six subjective criteria for weeding in the CREW model, and they are summed up by the acronym MUSTIE:

M = Misleading—factually inaccurate

U = Ugly—worn beyond mending or rebinding

S = Superseded—by a new edition or by a much better book on the subject

T = Trivial—of no discernible literary or scientific merit

I = Irrelevant to the needs and interests of the library's community

E = Elsewhere—the material is easily obtainable from another library

Sometimes you will see the acronym written as MUSTY, with a Y replacing the IE and indicating that *Your* collection has no need for this material because it is inappropriate for your users or not relevant to their needs. Either way, the acronym is easy to remember as you CREW!

GENERAL CRITERIA FOR WEEDING

Let's explore some of the general criteria, both objective and subjective, to consider when weeding.

Age. The age of the material is key. Using either the CREW guidelines or our recommended/maximum age in the chart in the appendix, you can determine whether something should be kept or tossed by age, meaning the number of years since the last copyright or since the publication date. Remember, these are general guidelines. Although theoretically this method is objective, you will need to use your professional judgment to determine how old is too old. Other factors will come into play here, including student access to other resources (online databases and full-text sources; a public library), the curriculum and use of library media materials in the subject area under consideration, budget for replacement materials, cooperative agreements with other school library media centers and other types of libraries, and the importance and use of the school library media center by the school community.

Use. Generally, if something has not circulated in three years, it is probably not worth keeping. Exceptions, of course, might be the reference collection in which materials do not circulate, AV materials that may get more use in the library media center, and other items that you find on tables and book carts that have been used but not checked out. You may want to mark those in some way as you reshelve to indicate that they have been used, when, and how often. Another possible exception is an item that may get more use if it is moved to another section of the shelves or made more accessible. Remember, duplicate copies may get less use, so eliminate some of those. Some topics are time-sensitive, and a lack of circulation may indicate the phase of interest or popularity has passed. If there are too many titles on a topic, keep the best. If there are items that seem to be useful and meet other criteria, you may decide to try promoting them before discarding them.

Physical Condition. Sometimes poor physical condition comes with age or use. In any case, consider weeding materials that are damaged or raggedy. If they are dirty, roach-eaten, or mildewed, if bindings are falling apart, if pages are yellowed, marked, or missing, the materials will not be used and need to be weeded. If they are worn from being used and loved, replace with a new copy or a newer edition.

Currency of Content. Toss any materials with outdated or obsolete information. Do not keep them for historical value. Instead, select materials that put the topic in perspective. Likewise, eliminate materials that reflect bias or stereotyping. Reconsider topics that were "hot" a few years ago, but are irrelevant or of little interest today. Consider the illustrations and photos. Are they dated?

Duplication. You may have duplicate copies of titles that were once popular but no longer in demand. Keep the best copy if it meets other criteria. If new editions have been published, keep the most recent. You may also have more titles than you need on any one topic; again, consider keeping only the best and most recent. If titles in some areas are not used very often, consider other sources of that information—the public library, interlibrary loan through consortia or district union catalogs, or online resources. Eliminate duplication wherever possible.

Curricular Integration. The first order of business in a school library media center is to support the curriculum. When the curriculum changes, so should the titles in the collection. Keep materials that are relevant to today's teaching methods and content. Prune the rest.

Appropriateness to the Collection. In addition to matching the curriculum, you will want materials that match your users and their needs. If your school demographics change, so should your collection. Struggling readers require more high-interest, lower reading-level books and fewer of the classics. Fewer students whose native language is other than English mean that fewer materials in other languages may be required. Deleting a course in babysitting or parenting from a high school curriculum may mean those picture books are no longer appropriate.

Bias. Weed anything that portrays bias on a topic unless there is a counterpoint title.

Obsolete Formats. Weed anything that is in a format that is no longer usable, such as 16 mm film, super 8 film loops, reel-to-reel tapes, beta tapes, 5.25-inch floppy disks (perhaps even 3.5-inch disks), and phonograph records. Depending upon the equipment you have, you may want to weed microfiche and microfilm if information is available online. Although you may still have filmstrip projectors that work, begin weeding filmstrips because of age and presentation format.

Here is a handy checklist of things to consider when weeding criteria.

Weeding Checklist

- [ ] How often has it been used in the last three years?
- [ ] Is it in poor physical condition?
- [ ] Does it contain inaccurate, outdated information?
- [ ] Is the tone condescending or biased?
- [ ] Does it promote stereotypes (gender, age, race, ethnic background, etc.)?
- [ ] Is the reading level appropriate for our students?
- [ ] Is it relevant to the curriculum?
- [ ] Is the format appropriate?
- [ ] Is it useful to students and classroom teachers?
- [ ] Is there another copy?
- [ ] Is there a newer edition?
- [ ] Is the information available in other formats?
- [ ] Is the information or title available in other locations?
- [ ] Is the information unique in any way?
- [ ] Is it listed in any current core collections, indexes, or recommended lists?
- [ ] Is it of local or regional interest?
- [ ] Is it an award winner or a classic?

ITEMS NOT TO WEED

Some materials are irreplaceable and should not be weeded unless they are unusable because of condition or accuracy. Do not remove the following.

Items with local or state history or interest. If you have collected items of interest to the population of your area—especially if it is a small town or an out-of-the-way place—consider saving them. Although they may not be of much interest to anyone else, these items should be retained for the community unless they are available at the public library. Similarly, titles by a local author, illustrator, or editor should be retained if they are used and in good condition. School yearbooks and annuals and other publications unique to the school should also remain in the collection. Titles set in your community or region may also be of special interest and should be retained.

Work of historical significance, including classics and award winners. These usually indicate high-quality writing and/or production values that endure the test of time. If in doubt, check with a book dealer or other reputable source.

Expensive titles. Unabridged dictionaries, titles that contain colored art plates, and other expensive titles should be retained as long as they are used and accurate.

Titles listed or indexed in current editions of the appropriate standard catalogs and quality bibliographic tools. You may want to check some titles against core collections and standard indexes. If they are listed there, consider keeping them or replacing them with newer editions. Before weeding anthologies of poetry, short stories, and plays, make sure the contents are available in other sources.

Special collections for cooperatives. Because of union catalogs, small budgets, magnet schools, and a new attitude toward resource sharing, some school library media centers have formed cooperative groups in which each participating library media center specializes in one or more sections of the collection. For example, a science and technology magnet would have larger and stronger collections in the 500s and 600s while another might focus on the arts or career education. If your library media center participates in such an arrangement, the collection must still be weeded for physical condition, accuracy, and relevance to the curriculum, but you must keep the needs of the other schools in mind. Duplicates may, in fact, be important, and more materials on each topic may be required.

HELPFUL HINTS

■ When a new edition supersedes an older one, discard the older one immediately. There is a new edition for a reason.

■ Pay attention to the textbook cycle in different subject areas in your school community. Generally, a new textbook will signal a review of curriculum-related titles, both print and nonprint. Often the review guidelines for new textbooks will give you good hints about the strengths and weaknesses of your collection in that area.

■ If most—but not all—of the work is outdated, remove it from the shelf. If the accurate portion is still useful, put the pages in the vertical file until the item can be replaced.

■ If AV items are shelved separately from print materials, be sure to weed the same Dewey numbers at the same time. Content criteria apply to both.

■ When in doubt about a content area, weed with teachers.

■ When in doubt about weeding the collection, ask for help from a colleague who has been successful.

■ Keep good examples of weeded titles to share with administrators, teachers, and parents to explain the need to weed.

Remember that you are the final decision maker when it comes to weeding. It is a professional responsibility.

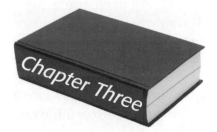

Chapter Three

Getting Started and Keeping On Keeping On

HOW TO START WEEDING

The most important step in weeding is to begin. Once you start, you'll see the benefits and you'll want to continue. But where should you start? It really doesn't matter as long as you do it. Here are some suggested starting points:

Begin with areas of curriculum change. If you are adding a new subject to the curriculum or if the curriculum is undergoing extensive revisions, this is a good place to start. If teachers are getting new textbooks, check your library's holdings in that subject area. Search your catalog for the range of Dewey numbers for the subject, then go to the shelves and pull each item. Check the publication date, the physical condition, and the photos and illustrations (see the general criteria in the previous chapter).

Begin with areas of current interest. What's in the news these days? War, hurricanes, poverty, elections, sporting events, the economy? Whatever it is, you can be sure your teachers and students are hearing about it. Does your collection provide adequate background information? Different points of view? In light of current information, is the collection accurate?

Begin with areas of the collection that get heavy use. The annual science fair is coming up and you know those materials will be in demand. Before the "crunch," review each item that might be used. Perhaps you know Mrs. K always does a unit on authors, and she asks the students to find and report some interesting facts about the author they have been assigned to research. Check your biography, autobiography, literature, and reference sections related to authors. With a few years' experience in a school, you can probably name the top ten topics. Start there.

Begin with areas in which you have interest and expertise. What are your hobbies? In what subjects are you most interested? Do you enjoy music? Start there. Are you a sports enthusiast? Have you always been excited about history? Do you love to travel? Whatever your interest, expertise, or passion, that is an excellent place to start weeding. With some knowledge of the subject area, you may feel more confident in tossing those out-of-date, inaccurate titles.

Pick a shelf at random. Start anywhere. Pick a shelf. You may be attracted to a particular shelf as a starting point because it is almost full and doing some weeding will give you some much-needed space. You may be attracted to an area that has been well used and appears to be a little messy. While straightening it out, examine the items. These are titles students have been using. Are the materials up to date and useful? You're reshelving materials that have been used during the day. You notice a title that is in tatters. Do you have enough other materials on the topic to justify weeding this item? Are they appropriate for your students, for your curriculum, for today?

Begin at the beginning. If you are more of a linear person, or if all else fails, start with the Dewey 000s and work through to the 900s. Then tackle the fiction section and the reference section and anything else that is left.

Weeding: Don't Put It Off!

Set Priorities
Not: I don't know where to begin, so I can't begin at all.
Not: I have to do it all! Nothing less will do.
Instead: The most important step is to pick one area I can focus on that is in need of weeding, review the weeding criteria for that topic, and get started.

Break the Task Down into Little Pieces
Not: There's so much to do and it's so time consuming. I'm overwhelmed.
Instead: I don't have to tackle the whole collection at once. I can begin with one section and schedule time to do more.

Set Up Small, Specific Goals
Not: I have to weed the collection this year.
Instead: If I weed a shelf a day, I can have the 200s weeded by Friday.

Take One Small Step at a Time
Not: There's too much to do. I'll never get it done.
Instead: What is on this shelf that needs to be reconsidered? I'll concentrate on that right now.

Reward Yourself Right Away When You Accomplish a Small Goal
Not: I can't take any time away from weeding until I'm all done.
Instead: I've weeded for an hour. Now I'll review those new videos.

(cont'd)

Use a Time Schedule

Not: I've got to devote the whole week after school is out to weeding.

Instead: I can use these times this week to weed: Monday, 10:00–10:30, Wednesday, 2:00–2:50, and Thursday, 1:30–2:15.

Learn How to Tell Time

Not: I don't have many biographies, so weeding those will be a snap. It won't take me more than an hour, so I can do it anytime.

Instead: Weeding a section usually takes a little longer than I expect, so I'll start tonight. I'll spend forty-five minutes reviewing the biography section.

Optimize Your Chances for Success

Not: I'll weed as soon as I get some help in the library media center.

Instead: I have good parent volunteers on Thursday afternoon. I'll weed then.

Not: It's just too hot in the library media center to weed this week; I'll wait until it gets cooler.

Instead: It's coolest in the library media center in the morning, so I'll do a little weeding each morning this week. (Choose whatever conditions are optimal for you to get work done.)

Delegate if Possible

Not: I'm the only person who can weed this collection.

Instead: I don't have to do this all by myself. I can ask teachers to help with some of the topics I'm weeding, since they are experts on the curriculum and content. Students can record titles to be deleted from the catalog. I can use volunteers to stamp the discards and box them.

Just Get Started

Not: I can't weed until I feel like it. I need to be motivated.

Instead: I will weed one topic each week starting today.

Look at What You Have Accomplished

Not: I've hardly made a dent in all that needs to be done.

Instead: I've finished weeding the history section. I've found some real gems that aren't being used and discovered some holes in the collection. The shelves look so much better when there is a little more space, and the whole section looks more inviting with the raggedy old volumes removed.

Be Realistic!

Not: I should be able to weed without interruption for a few days. How else will it ever get done?

Instead: I have lots of things to do that are important, and weeding is one of them. I'll do what I can this week and schedule my time so that I have time to plan with teachers and work on the research skills unit. I know there will be interruptions, but I will do what I can because a quality collection is so important to meeting the needs of students and teachers, and weeding is part of that.

Adapted from *Techniques to Manage Procrastination* from the Student Learning Center, CalREN Project, University of California, Berkeley.

WHEN TO WEED

Except for obvious weeds, we recommend that you do not weed during your first year in a school or in the school's library media center. Yes, you can toss titles that are roach-eaten or moldy, and if and when you spot information that is biased or totally inaccurate, it should go. (Does anyone really need a copy of a filmstrip called *The Soviet Union Today*, published in 1962? Not only are filmstrips obsolete but so is the information!)

It takes a while to get to know the curriculum, teaching needs and methods, the school community, and users' expectations for the collection. You'll begin to see areas where the collection is weak because you'll be asked for things you can't provide and may have to borrow via interlibrary loan, or you might have to refer students to the public library. You'll also identify areas of strength. You'll begin to recognize teachers who may have great interest in resource-based teaching or project-based learning and rely on library media resources. They'll be the ones you want to begin working with on your weeding project, and they can help you even in your first year.

Weed. I'm not telling you again!

—Doug Johnson, "Weed!"
(http://www.doug-johnson.com/
dougwri/weed.html)

Some people like "condensed weeding"; that is, they like to weed at one time of the year. Some do it before school begins. Others take a few days during the year—perhaps when schoolwide testing is going on in classrooms. Others like to do it at the same time as the inventory because items will only need to be handled one time, although with the magic of technology and barcode readers, there may be less hands-on examination of resources than there used to be.

We find it easier to weed a little bit at a time throughout the year, and that's the whole idea behind this book. You should establish a schedule and keep track of your progress. You may want to do a shelf a week or a topic every two weeks. Depending upon your instructional schedule, your library media center staffing, and your need to weed, you should establish a plan, write it down, let it be known to others, and—most importantly—stick with it. You will want to avoid weeding a section during times users are most likely to need it (holiday titles during holiday seasons, for example). You also know the times of the school year when you and the collection get the most use. Don't schedule any weeding for those times. That way you won't have to reschedule!

Use your lesson plan book or calendar to establish a realistic weeding schedule. Make weeding a high priority. Most collections should be weeded once a year. If your collection hasn't been weeded for a while, it might take longer the first time. Even in small school library media centers, it may take two or three years to cover the entire collection, but with a firm schedule, it will be done.

Obvious weeds should be removed whenever they are identified. If you find a book that has missing pages or a faded, ragged cover, and it can't be (or shouldn't be) repaired, weed it immediately. Don't reshelve it and wait until that topic is scheduled to be weeded. As you are gathering materials for a teacher with whom you are planning, think about accuracy, condition, and general usefulness. If the item can't pass your established criteria, weed it when you see it.

As well as establishing a written schedule, you should record the results of your weeding.

- What awful things did you find? (You can laugh about these later.)
- How many items were weeded?
- How many duplicates were eliminated?
- What ideas for new materials came to you as you examined your current collection?
- What is the priority for purchases in this area?
- Where could you look and to whom could you talk to get an idea of the needs in this area and to identify quality materials?
- Can students access information online for this topic? Do they?

This written record comes in handy when talking to your administrator about your accomplishments during the year and your budget needs as well. Your notes can help when it is time to purchase new materials, and they can be useful if anyone challenges your decisions. Finally, just reviewing your weeding record can fill you with pride in a job well done and motivate you to do more. With a schedule and a record of your progress, you'll always know where you've been and where you're going.

WHEN IS WEEDING COMPLETED?

Weeding is an ongoing task. Even if you decide to weed the entire collection once a year, it will need to be done the next year—and probably before that. Just as you are always mindful of items and topics that need to be added to the collection, you'll learn to be aware that weeding is always needed. As items circulate, take a few moments to look at them closely. As you reshelve materials, keep weeding criteria in mind.

Curriculum changes. Student needs, abilities, and interests change. Teaching methods evolve. Society's needs and expectations for our students change each year. Current events demand new materials, and historical events and titles need to be examined with perspective. AV formats become obsolete. As a result, weeding is a professional challenge, and the task is never completed.

WORKING WITH TEACHERS AND OTHERS

The school library media center exists for the entire school community, so it makes sense to involve them in the weeding process. This includes administrators, teachers, clerks and aides, volunteers, custodians, parents, and students. Show them some really good examples of "bad" things in your collection. Tell them how weeding benefits the collection. Show them this book, if necessary, to drive home the fact that this is a professional responsibility. Show them your collection development policy and the section about weeding, assuring them that both are critical to the mission of the school library media program. Communicating the importance of weeding to all these groups may save you time and trouble later, and, more importantly, garner support for the budget to replace materials and expand the collection with new titles.

Always inform your principal and other administrators when you prepare to do a major, formal weeding. It's a great opportunity to help him or her understand your role as a professional and the importance of the library media program to the instructional goals of the school. Teachers, custodians, parents, and others will lend support instead of create opposition when they understand what you are doing and why.

Teachers can be some of your best friends when it comes to weeding specific areas. Who knows the biology curriculum better than the biology teacher? Set aside some time to work with one or more teachers to weed a section that is important to them. Invite them to a "weeding party"—just a few teachers at a time. Again, explain the benefits of weeding and talk about general criteria; let them help develop specific criteria for their subject area and then examine the materials in that area.

As the teachers review the materials, ask them to mark in some way the items that they'd like you to reexamine or that they'd recommend withdrawing from the collection. They can use colored bookmarks or removable spine dots or just turn items spine down on the shelf—anything to indicate to you that these items are suspect.

Depending upon the subject, the teachers available to help, their attitudes toward the library media program and weeding, and their time, you may want to first weed a section yourself and then ask for their help. Ask them to look at items about which you are unsure and to use their expertise to evaluate the accuracy of the content, its appropriateness for students, and its relevance to the curriculum.

WEEDING TOPICS, CRITERIA, AND SUGGESTIONS

Wherever you start, you'll want to refer to the general weeding criteria in chapter 2 and to the heart of this book, the topics with specific criteria in chapter 4. For example, you know the World Series is coming up—or spring training—or you hear that fantasy baseball is popular with your students. This is a perfect time to reexamine your baseball collection.

The topics in chapter 4 are in general Dewey order (although some topics include more than one Dewey number). A chart in the appendix lists all the topics, a suggested minimum and maximum number of years to keep information in specific Dewey ranges, and notes for those Dewey ranges. Each topic in chapter 4 includes the following.

General Weeding Guidelines: What are the recommendations for weeding according to the age of the publication in each area? We generally provide a range for each Dewey number included in the topic. However, please keep in mind that these are very broad and very liberal. Depending upon your collection, a range of five to fifteen years can become six or maybe even twelve. That is for you to decide. Depending upon the "chaff in your wheat"—the condition of your collection and length of time since the last weeding—you may want to be more conservative. Only in very rare instances, however, should the age of an item exceed the recommended guidelines.

A Rationale for Weeding: Why weed baseball, for example? Because it is an area that attracts many readers, including perhaps struggling readers who have a passion for sports. Students play ball at recess and during physical education classes, but they also play after school, and many keep track of their local or favorite teams and players.

Dewey Numbers to Check: The primary Dewey number for baseball is 796, but you'll also want to think "baseball" as you review biographies and fiction titles with a baseball theme. Remember to check your AV titles in this area, too.

Specific Criteria for Weeding: Here are guidelines to keep in mind as you reconsider items on this topic. Some kids are baseball fanatics, and they will recognize errors and inconsistencies. That may teach them to distrust all the information on your shelves. Watch out for the gender and racial stereotypes that have been prevalent in sports. Sometimes these will be blatantly apparent as you review the titles and content, but frequently bias may appear in more subtle ways such as in illustrations, photos, or tone.

Tips for Replacing Titles: These are points to keep in mind as you look for new materials on this topic. Look for biographies of popular new players that students hold in high regard. Think about related materials as well. For example, be sure you have materials to satisfy curiosity piqued by the current steroid controversy.

Consider Weeding Titles Like These: Here we list specific titles and publication dates of items you might have on your shelves—and probably shouldn't keep. If you don't have any of these titles, good! But that doesn't mean you don't have titles that should be weeded. Reading through the list of titles and looking at the dates will give you a good idea of the kinds of materials at which you might want to take a closer look. The list will also raise points to think about in this section of the collection. For example, here are several titles from the baseball list with examples of what they made us think about:

- *Baseball for Boys*, 1960 (Baseball is also for girls! Do illustrations include out-of-date, unappealing clothing? Do illustrations reflect the diversity in today's society and reflect the values we are trying to instill in our students?)
- *Baseball's Great Moments*, 1975 (There have been so many great moments since 1975! And none of these happened in our students' lifetimes.)
- *Baseball's Greatest All-Star Games*, 1979 (We've had almost thirty years of All-Star Games! We bet there were some "greatest" among those as well.)
- *Baseball's Greatest Players Today*, 1963 (Those players are now retired or maybe dead! Kids won't care about most of them.)
- *Baseball's Ten Greatest Pitchers*, 1979 (Students will probably be able to name quite a few pitchers who are as good as if not better than these ten.)
- *Careers in Baseball*, 1973 (Most careers that still exist have undergone dramatic changes in pay, educational requirements, use of technology, and more. Some careers no longer exist [perhaps the local stadium organist] and other opportunities have developed [webmaster for a team, psychological sports coach].)

Each of the seventy-one topics in chapter 4 includes the same sections. Review the information provided on the topic you are going to weed before you begin. Keep the book with you and open to the topic as you pull and review items. If you have helpers, talk to them about the kinds of things for which you will be looking. You may also want to refer to the chart in the appendix for other recommendations.

Let no book remain on the shelves unless someone fights to keep it there. Let an undefended book be a condemned book. This must be the accepted philosophy of the library. Gone must be the static conception of the library as a storage organ, and in its place we must conceive of the library as a dynamic circulatory system, a channel through which books pass on their way from the publisher to the incinerator.

—G. Hardin, "Doctrine of Sufferance in the Library," *College and Research Libraries* 8 (April 1947)

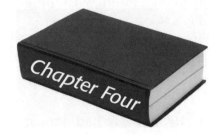

Chapter Four

Weeding Criteria by Topic and Dewey Number

Time to get busy!

In this chapter, you'll find seventy-one topics for weeding. Although this won't include the entire collection, it will hit most of the topics about which your students and teachers want and need information. Once you finish a section, you may be so pleased that you'll want to keep going by weeding a little to the left and a little to the right of the area you just finished. Go ahead!

For each topic, we give you general weeding guidelines by age of the publication, a rationale for weeding this particular topic, Dewey numbers to check (some topics can be found in more than one Dewey number or range of numbers), and specific criteria for weeding. In addition, we offer suggestions for replacing titles and provide a sample of items (from real school catalogs) whose titles or dates of publication or both suggest they deserve serious consideration when weeding. Please remember, these are not the *only* titles that need reevaluation, but we list them to put you in the right frame of mind before beginning.

On most pages you'll find some white space. Feel free to jot down items you've weeded, titles that need weeding next time around, or ideas that come to you while weeding.

The topics, in Dewey order, are listed below.

Primary Dewey Number	Weeding Topic	Primary Dewey Number	Weeding Topic
001.9	Curiosities and Wonders	305.4	Women's Issues
004	Computer Science	321.8	Democracy
025	Libraries and Librarians	322	Terrorism
170	Moral Education	323	Civil Rights
200	Religion	324	Presidential Elections
301	Black History	325	Immigration
302	Conflict Management	330	Personal Finance

Primary Dewey Number	Weeding Topic	Primary Dewey Number	Weeding Topic
331	Careers	740	Hobbies and Crafts
332	The Stock Market	741	Drawing and Cartooning
360	Drug and Alcohol Education	770	Photography
362.4	Disabilities	780	Music
363.2	Forensic Science	792.8	Dance
370	Education	796	Sports
380	Transportation	796.357	Baseball
392	Dating and Courtship	796.48	Olympic Games
394	Holidays	808	Poetry
398	Folktales	808.7	Wit and Humor
400	Languages	822.3	Shakespeare
507.8	Science Experiments	910	Geography
510	Mathematics	920	Biography
520	Space and Astronomy	940	Europe
551.2	Earthquakes and Volcanoes	940.53	The Holocaust
551.6	Weather	940.53	World War II
567.9	Dinosaurs	947	Russia
576	Genetic Engineering	959.7	Vietnam
576.8	Evolution	960	Africa
577	Ecology	970.004	Native Americans
597	Reptiles and Amphibians	971–972	Canada and Mexico
600	Vocational Trades	972.91	Cuba
613.2	Nutrition	973	U.S. Presidents
613.7	Physical Fitness	973.7	The Civil War
613.85	Tobacco Education	973.93	September 11
614.5	AIDS	FIC	Fiction
616	Diseases	REF	Reference
629.1	Aviation History	SC	Short Stories
641.5	Cooking		

001.9
Curiosities and Wonders

Why Weed Curiosities and Wonders?

Titles on the subject of curiosities and wonders attract a broad range of students, from the most avid reader to the most reluctant. These titles will circulate! But outdated content will quickly be a negative reflection on your collection when detected by the reader. Weed this topic so your students won't find information on some curiosity or wonder that is no longer curious or wondrous!

Dewey Numbers to Check

The majority of items to be reviewed on this topic will be found in the 001.9s (Controversial Knowledge) and the 031–032.02s (Books of Miscellaneous Facts). However, you may also have titles of this type scattered across the collection with their subject areas, such as the sciences. Also, remember to check the reference and AV collections.

Specific Criteria for Weeding

Because titles in this subject area tend to be heavy circulators, first look for books or AV items that are in poor physical shape. Replace as necessary. Next, look at the publication dates and think in terms of the expansion of knowledge since 1975 or even 1985! Many things that might have been unexplained twenty or thirty years ago are commonplace today.

Also, look for titles with any underlying gender bias, such as those implying (maybe just by illustrations) that only boys are curious about the wonders of such subject areas as science or inventions.

Tips for Replacing Titles

When replacing or adding new titles, try to find books with high visual appeal to attract reluctant readers.

Consider Weeding Titles Like These

- [ ] *Bees Can't Fly, but They Do: Things That Are Still a Mystery to Science*, 1976
- [ ] *The Bermuda Triangle and Other Mysteries of Nature*, 1980
- [ ] *The Biggest, Smallest, Fastest, Tallest Things You've Ever Heard Of*, 1980
- [ ] *The Book of Facts and Records*, 1977
- [ ] *The Book of Firsts*, 1974
- [ ] *The Boys' Book of Engineering Wonders of the World*, 1961
- [ ] *The Boys' Book of Modern Chemical Wonders*, 1966
- [ ] *Children's Guide to Knowledge: Wonders of Nature, Marvels of Science and Man*, 1971
- [ ] *The Curious Book: Fascinating Facts about People, Places, and Things*, 1976
- [ ] *Enigmas and Mysteries*, 1976
- [ ] *Extraterrestrial Intervention: The Evidence*, 1974
- [ ] *Forgotten Worlds: Scientific Secrets of the Ancients and Their Warning for Our Time*, 1973
- [ ] *The Illustrated Book of World Records*, 1974
- [ ] *Investigating the Unexplained: A Compendium of Disquieting Mysteries of the Natural World*, 1972

- [ ] *Missing! Stories of Strange Disappearances*, 1979
- [ ] *Monsters and Other Science Mysteries* [filmstrip], 1977
- [ ] *More Oddities and Enigmas*, 1973
- [ ] *Myths of the Space Age*, 1967
- [ ] *Oddities: A Book of Unexplained Facts*, 1965
- [ ] *Strange Phenomena* [filmstrip], 1972
- [ ] *Strange Stories, Amazing Facts: Stories That Are Bizarre, Unusual, Odd, Astonishing, and Often Incredible*, 1967
- [ ] *Ten Thousand Wonderful Things: Comprising Whatever Is Marvelous and Rare, Curious, Eccentric and Extraordinary in All Ages and Nations*, 1970
- [ ] *This Baffling World*, 1968
- [ ] *Unexplained Facts: Enigmas and Curiosities*, 1965
- [ ] *You'd Better Believe It: Fascinating Facts and Feats*, 1980

004
Computer Science

GENERAL WEEDING GUIDELINES

000s
5 to 10 years

600s
5 to 15 years

Why Weed Computer Science?

A world that calmly accepts the fact that computer hardware is obsolete shortly after purchase should also understand the need to weed the subject area of computer science in library media collections. Dated computer literature is just as obsolete as a piece of discarded hardware.

Dewey Numbers to Check

Materials on computer science will be found in all these Dewey areas: 004–006s (Data Processing, Computer Programming, Special Computer Methods), 370s (Education), 620s (Engineering and Allied Operations), and 650s (Management). If you have an automated catalog with keyword searching, truncation, and publication date limiting, you can easily locate most of the older titles on computer science. Check the AV titles also that result from your search. Although fiction titles are not always given computer science subject headings that will help you in a search, watch for items that could contain misleading information.

Specific Criteria for Weeding

Consider the types of computer hardware in your school. You will want to retain materials about computers that are still used in your school. Consider weeding books and AV materials pertaining to hardware no longer in your school or not likely to be used by students in their homes.

Then consider the curriculum. What technology skills are integrated into the curriculum? Which of those skills are the students and staff expected to master? Does your school offer classes in computer programming? If so, which programming languages are taught? Weed items that no longer support the curriculum. Eliminate titles that support out-of-date software titles and versions. Consider checking with the faculty sponsors of any computer clubs at your school to help identify items that are too outdated for the computer hobbyist.

The outlook for computer careers changes dramatically in just a few years. Beware of computer history books that stop years ago. Even books about networks, e-mail, and the Internet may be outdated if they are more than two or three years old.

Tips for Replacing Titles

Although new computer science developments and uses usually beat the publishing market, try to locate titles in areas of new interest (weblogs, podcasts, and RSS, for example). This is a good time to listen to your students and staff techies to identify new areas of interest.

Consider Weeding Titles Like These

- [ ] *80 Practical Time-Saving Programs for the TRS-80*, 1982
- [ ] *The A to Z Book of Computer Games*, 1979
- [ ] *The ABC of Basic: An Introduction to Programming for Librarians*, 1982
- [ ] *All About Computers* [filmstrip], 1981
- [ ] *Are You Computer Literate?* 1979
- [ ] *Careers in Computer Science and Service* [videorecording], 1982
- [ ] *Communications in the World of the Future*, 1969
- [ ] *Computer Hardware: What It Is and How It Works* [videorecording], 1982
- [ ] *The Computer Survival Handbook: How to Talk Back to Your Computers*, 1979
- [ ] *Computers: Tools for Today*, 1972
- [ ] *Disk Operating System Instructional and Reference Manual: Do's and Don'ts of DOS; A Manual for Using the Apple Disk II with DOS Version 3.2*, 1979
- [ ] *Getting Involved with Your Own Computer: A Guide for Beginners*, 1977
- [ ] *Hackers: Heroes of the Computer Revolution*, 1968

- [ ] *How to Cope in a Computer Age without Pulling the Plug*, 1971
- [ ] *Information Systems in the 80's: Products, Markets, and Vendors*, 1982
- [ ] *Introduction to the Computer: The Tool of Business*, 1977
- [ ] *Personal Computers: What They Are and How to Use Them*, 1978
- [ ] *School Administrator's Introduction to Instructional Use of Computers*, 1982
- [ ] *Security of Computer Systems*, 1972
- [ ] *The Selection of Local Area Computer Networks*, 1982
- [ ] *Standard Dictionary of Computers and Information Processing*, 1977
- [ ] *Those Amazing Computers! Uses of Modern Thinking Machines*, 1973
- [ ] *Understanding Computers*, 1967
- [ ] *What Computers Can't Do: The Limits of Artificial Intelligence*, 1979
- [ ] *Your Career in Computer Programming*, 1967

025
Libraries and Librarians

Why Weed Libraries and Librarians?

Libraries and librarians are supposed to be proficient in weeding, but are they weeding titles on libraries and librarians? You and your library media center may be modeling current professionalism, but your collection titles on that topic could be giving a different impression.

Dewey Numbers to Check

Check your shelves from 025 (Operation of Libraries) through 028 (Reading and Use of Other Information Media). Also look at the 011s (Bibliographies) for any bibliographies that feature research and reference techniques. There may be only one or two titles in your reference collection, but definitely check the AV area for titles outdated in both content and format. The fiction section (and Es for lower grades) may also have titles that are neither popular nor accurate in portraying libraries and librarians.

An important area to check is your professional collection, probably the home to many titles so old as to no longer be of use by today's professionals.

Specific Criteria for Weeding

This should be a very easy topic for you to weed since *you* are the expert in what librarians do now and what a modern library media center is like today. The hard part will be for you to separate sentimentally from a view of libraries that may have initially attracted you to the profession years ago. Think of what today's students should know about libraries and the profession, and remove older, misleading titles from your database.

Methods of library research have changed drastically in recent decades. Outdated titles must be removed to effectively teach information literacy. Developing a love of reading is not served by having unattractive titles on using books and libraries.

Tips for Replacing Titles

Replace old formats (filmstrips!) with new approaches (such as graphic novels) and try to add titles that connect subjects of popular or current interest to libraries, books, and reading.

Consider Weeding Titles Like These

- *ABCs of Library Promotion*, 1980
- *Adventures on Library Shelves*, 1968
- *Applying the New Copyright Law: A Guide for Educators and Librarians*, 1979
- *AV Cataloging and Processing Simplified*, 1971
- *Basic Library Skills*, 1979
- *A Book to Begin on Libraries*, 1964
- *Books and the Teenage Reader: A Guide for Teachers, Librarians, and Parents*, 1980
- *Building Ethnic Collections: An Annotated Guide for School Media Centers and Public Libraries*, 1977
- *Careers in a Library*, 1978
- *Choosing an Automated Library System: A Planning Guide*, 1980
- *Computer Systems in the Library: A Handbook for Managers and Designers*, 1973
- *Creating a School Library Media Program*, 1973
- *Dewey Decimal Classification* [filmstrip], 1979
- *Finding Facts Fast: How to Find Out What You Want and Need to Know*, 1979
- *Guide to the Use of Books and Libraries*, 1979
- *Guide to Writing a Research Paper* [filmstrip], 1979
- *Hooray for the Library* [filmstrip], 1977
- *How to Survive in School: Using Library Resources and Reference Materials* [filmstrip], 1979
- *How to Use Reference Materials*, 1980
- *I Want to Be a Librarian*, 1960
- *The Library: What's in It for You?* [filmstrip], 1975
- *Meet the Card Catalog* [filmstrip], 1979
- *The Reference Section* [videorecording], 1980
- *Using the Library*, 1985
- *What Happens at the Library*, 1971

GENERAL WEEDING
GUIDELINES

100s
5 to 10 years

300s
5 to 20 years

170
Moral Education

Why Weed Moral Education?

Aside from the question of whose job it is (home, church, or school) to teach ethics and morality is the reality that there are titles on this topic in every school library media center. If you have them, you must also weed and replace them to keep the collection current.

Dewey Numbers to Check

Most of the titles in this subject area will be found in the 170s (Ethics). You may also have titles that cover this subject in the 150s (Psychology), the beginning of the 300s (Social Sciences), and in the 370s (Education). Overall, you will most likely find the bulk of these titles in the professional and AV collections, but remember to also check the general and reference collections.

Specific Criteria for Weeding

Although the basic message of morality and ethics may stay very close to the same over the generations, the trappings of those messages become critical in reaching the intended audience. Today's students may not recognize a peer pressure situation if it is dressed in the fashions of the 1960s and 1970s—especially if it is represented as current by the title or the narrator. Test your titles by ignoring the content and looking just at the visuals.

Specific moral choices and decisions have changed drastically over the years. For example, access to computers and the Internet has had a great impact on the ethical decisions students make when completing homework and projects for school. Our global community expands students' range of choices and experiences, both the good and the bad. Check your titles to see if they accurately reflect the world of today.

Tips for Replacing Titles

Although it is tempting to purchase titles with current sports or music personalities speaking out on this topic, be prepared to reconsider keeping the title if a future controversy involving that person would compromise the message. Unfortunately, it happens. In the 300s, be sure you have titles that discuss present-day ethical situations, such as computer hacking, spam, and computer crime.

Consider Weeding Titles Like These

☐ *As Others See You: Creating a Reputation* [videorecording], 1981

☐ *Be the Best You Can Be,* 1985

☐ *Blueprint for Teenage Living,* 1958

☐ *But It Isn't Yours* [filmstrip], 1972

☐ *Caring: A Feminine Approach to Ethics and Moral Education,* 1984

☐ *Contemporary Moral Issues,* 1974

☐ *Coping with Peer Pressure: Getting Along without Going Along* [videorecording], 1976

☐ *The Corrupted Land: The Social Morality of Modern America,* 1967

☐ *Crises Youth Face Today,* 1973

☐ *The Culture of Narcissism: American Life in an Age of Diminishing Expectations,* 1978

☐ *Dare to Be Different: Dealing with Peer Pressure,* 1980

☐ *Deciding Right from Wrong: The Dilemma of Morality Today* [filmstrip], 1974

☐ *Developing Self-Respect* [filmstrip], 1981

☐ *The Development of Motives and Values in the Child,* 1964

☐ *Donald Duck's Elementary Guidance Series* [filmstrip], 1977

☐ *First Things: The Trouble with Truth* [filmstrip], 1972

☐ *Helping Children Accept Themselves and Others,* 1956

☐ *It's Up to You* [filmstrip], 1972

☐ *Life Goals: Setting Personal Priorities* [filmstrip], 1976

☐ *Making Value Judgments: Decisions for Today,* 1972

☐ *The School's Role as Moral Authority,* 1977

☐ *Sex and the New Morality,* 1968

☐ *The Teenager and the New Morality,* 1970

☐ *Turning Points: New Developments, New Directions in Value Clarification,* 1978

☐ *Values, Rights, and the New Morality: Do They Conflict?* 1977

GENERAL WEEDING GUIDELINES

200s
10 to 15 years

200
Religion

Why Weed Religion?

The religion section of most school library media centers may seem small and relatively inactive compared to the rest of the collection. Why bother to weed? Because different religions and religious beliefs are in the news today, and students need current, unbiased information in these sensitive times. Your students may turn to your collection to try to understand current conflicts and issues. Weed any old and misleading titles and offer your users attractive works with a contemporary perspective.

Dewey Numbers to Check

The 200 (Religion) section will probably be small enough that you can review all materials to identify any titles to weed. Review the reference section and check the AV collection for older titles as well as outdated formats.

Specific Criteria for Weeding

Begin by applying the standard of physical condition to titles in the religion section. Look at the overall condition of each title. Because this section usually doesn't circulate heavily, physical wear and tear might not be as obvious as other conditions, such as smell and feel. You might have to pick up the book and do the sniff test!

Next, look at the content of each title. You probably have some weighty encyclopedias or atlases of religion, but if they are from the 1970s or 1980s (or even earlier!), they should be replaced with a newer edition. Any work that professes to address the beliefs of "today's" youth must be a current publication. If the title implies that the content is a review of contemporary religious life and thought, be sure it was published within the last ten years. Then review the topics covered to make sure they appeal to students today.

Finally, look at format in the AV collection. That old filmstrip surveying the world's religions might be in good shape, but it must be discarded.

Tips for Replacing Titles

In the years since September 11, many books and AV materials have been published that address contemporary religious issues of interest to many students today. Be sure the wide range of world religions is represented because students will hear about many different religions on the news, and with today's diverse population, these religions most likely are represented in your community.

Consider Weeding Titles Like These

- [ ] *As Christians Face Rival Religions: An Inter-Religious Strategy for Community without Compromise*, 1962
- [ ] *By These Faiths: Religions for Today*, 1977
- [ ] *A Dictionary of Comparative Religion*, 1970
- [ ] *The Encyclopedia of American Religions*, 1978
- [ ] *The Essential Unity of All Religions*, 1966
- [ ] *The Faiths of Mankind: A Guide to the World's Living Religions*, 1964
- [ ] *The Future of Religions*, 1966
- [ ] *Great Religions of the World*, 1978
- [ ] *Gurus, Swamis, and Avatars: Spiritual Masters and Their American Disciples*, 1972
- [ ] *The Heathens: Primitive Man and His Religions*, 1948
- [ ] *Introduction to Asian Religions*, 1957
- [ ] *Major World Religions: Religions of East Asia; Taoism, Confucianism and Shintoism* [filmstrip], 1978
- [ ] *Many People, Many Faiths: An Introduction to the Religious Life of Mankind*, 1976
- [ ] *Minority Religions in America*, 1972
- [ ] *Modern Trends in World Religions*, 1959
- [ ] *New Gods in America: An Informal Investigation into the New Religions of American Youth Today*, 1971
- [ ] *Religion in the Middle East: Three Religions in Concord and Conflict*, 1969
- [ ] *Religions Around the World* [filmstrip], 1975
- [ ] *Religions in America: A Completely Revised and Up-to-Date Guide to Churches and Religious Groups in the United States*, 1963
- [ ] *Religions of America: Ferment and Faith in an Age of Crisis; A New Guide and Almanac*, 1975
- [ ] *Strange Sects and Curious Cults*, 1961
- [ ] *Understanding the New Religions*, 1978
- [ ] *What the Great Religions Believe*, 1963
- [ ] *What's the Difference? A Comparison of the Faiths Men Live By*, 1965
- [ ] *Young People and Religions*, 1970

301
Black History

GENERAL WEEDING GUIDELINES

300s
5 to 20 years

900s
5 to 15 years

Biography
5 to 10 years

Why Weed Black History?

Black History Month, observed in February each year, will almost certainly tax the resources of any library media center. You may be reluctant to discard any title regardless of age or condition. But the heavy use is the very reason you must weed to prevent the extensive exposure of inappropriate or physically unattractive titles. Weed and add some new titles each year before the national observance of Black History Month.

Dewey Numbers to Check

You will have to check several areas of your collection for this subject. Review the 300s from 301 (Sociology and Anthropology) through 328 (The Legislative Process). Check the 750s (Painting and Paintings), 780s (Music), and 790s (Recreational and Performing Arts) for famous black achievers. The 900s will require checks in the 960s (History of Africa) as well as 973s (United States). Biographies, both collective (920) and individual, should also be included in your review. Finally, check your fiction, reference, and AV sections.

Specific Criteria for Weeding

Weeding black history titles requires a little knowledge about the beginning of this observance. In 1926 Carter Godwin Woodson founded Negro History Week, which was changed to Black History Month in 1976. Political correctness of terminology does not require you to weed such primary source materials as *The Mis-Education of the Negro*, written by Woodson in 1933. But if you still have an edition of this title published in the 1930s or 1940s, you should replace it with a more recent edition.

Take a hard look at any older titles that imply current thought and attitudes. Weed any that are offensive or incorrect. Review biographical materials and keep only those that have either popular appeal or historical significance.

Tips for Replacing Titles

Because Black History Month was established to recognize African American contributions to society in all fields of endeavor, be sure that your collection reflects a wide range of contributions, not just popular figures in sports and entertainment. For example, do you have a biography of Carter Godwin Woodson? You should.

Consider Weeding Titles Like These

- *100 Amazing Facts about the Negro: With Complete Proof,* 1970
- *An American Dilemma: The Negro Problem and Modern Democracy,* 1962
- *An American Traveler's Guide to Black History,* 1968
- *Black African Literature in English since 1952,* 1967
- *Black America Yesterday and Today* [picture], 1969
- *Black American English: Its Background and Its Usage in the Schools and in Literature,* 1975
- *Black American Music: Past and Present,* 1985
- *The Black Athlete: Emergence and Arrival,* 1968
- *Black Heroes in World History,* 1968
- *Black History: A Reappraisal,* 1968
- *The Black Odyssey: Migration to the Cities* [filmstrip], 1970
- *Black Protest: History, Documents, and Analyses; 1619 to the Present,* 1968
- *An Introduction to Black Literature in America: From 1746 to the Present,* 1968
- *The Music of Black Americans,* 1983
- *The Negro Impact on Western Civilization,* 1970
- *The Negro in Contemporary American Literature,* 1928
- *The Negro in the Armed Forces: His Value and Status, Past, Present, and Potential,* 1945
- *Negro Musicians and Their Music,* 1936
- *Neo-African Literature: A History of Black Writing,* 1969
- *The New Negro of the South: A Portrait of Movements and Leadership,* 1967
- *Pictorial History of the Black American,* 1968
- *Story of the Negro,* 1955
- *They Showed the Way: Forty American Negro Leaders,* 1964
- *The Tuskegee Airmen: The Story of the Negro in the U.S. Air Force,* 1955
- *World's Great Men of Color,* 1979

302
Conflict Management

Why Weed Conflict Management?

The nature and ramifications of conflict in today's schools have changed drastically in the past few years. You should carefully examine materials published as recently as only five years ago. This won't be a difficult job because you probably have very few older titles on this subject. But if you do, now is the time to replace them. There are many new and relevant titles—another sign of the times.

Dewey Numbers to Check

Any old print materials on conflict management in your general collection will be found in the 302s (Social Interaction) and 303s (Social Processes). You are more likely to find out-of-date materials on this subject in the professional and AV collections. The fiction section may also have a few titles that should be reviewed.

Specific Criteria for Weeding

We all experienced some bullying or teasing in our school years, but few of us endured the school violence that today's students are exposed to—personally or secondhand via the media. School-yard bullying and teasing now often result in deadly confrontations or retaliations. Yesterday's recommendations for dealing with the school bully could be dangerous today.

Professional and AV collections will probably also have materials that don't apply to today's problems. If unused, they are deadweight on the shelves. If used, their information could cause more harm than good. Weed them.

Tips for Replacing Titles

Over the years, there have always been students from less than ideal home situations, but a growing number of today's students are experiencing home lives that include great stress and violence. We are also seeing more students whose families seem to be indifferent to or detached from their children's lives and emotions. Try to provide current and realistic materials that will assist those students in dealing with their anger and aggressive behavior. Also, be sure you have materials with appropriate responses for today's victims of bullying.

Consider Weeding Titles Like These

- [ ] *The Adolescent Experience: Interpersonal Relationships* [filmstrip], 1973
- [ ] *Aggression, Hostility, and Anxiety in Children*, 1953
- [ ] *Aggress-less: How to Turn Anger and Aggression into Positive Action*, 1982
- [ ] *Approaching Potentially Explosive Conflicts* [motion picture], 1976
- [ ] *Conflict and Decision: Analyzing Educational Issues*, 1972
- [ ] *Conflict Resolution: An Elementary School Curriculum*, 1990
- [ ] *Creative Conflict Resolution: More Than 200 Activities for Keeping Peace in the Classroom*, 1984
- [ ] *A Curriculum on Conflict Management: Practical Methods for Helping Children Explore Creative Alternatives in Dealing with Conflict*, 1975
- [ ] *Fighting, Bullying, Gossiping, and Teasing People* [filmstrip], 1981
- [ ] *Getting Along with Your Teachers*, 1981
- [ ] *How to Turn War into Peace: A Child's Guide to Conflict Resolution*, 1979
- [ ] *Human Being: How to Have a Creative Relationship Instead of a Power Struggle*, 1974

- [ ] *Kindle Getting Along: Concept of Relationships with Others* [filmstrip], 1972
- [ ] *Learning the Skills of Peacemaking: An Activity Guide for Elementary-Age Children on Communicating, Cooperating, Resolving Conflict*, 1987
- [ ] *Lessons in Conflict Resolution*, 1990
- [ ] *Managing Conflict: A Curriculum for Adolescents*, 1989
- [ ] *New Ways of Managing Conflict*, 1976
- [ ] *Nobody Likes a Bully* [videorecording], 1979
- [ ] *Peacemaking Skills for Little Kids* [sound recording], 1988
- [ ] *Resolving Classroom Conflict*, 1974
- [ ] *Violence! Our Fastest-Growing Public Health Problem*, 1984
- [ ] *Why Is Everybody Always Picking on Me? A Guide to Handling Bullies for Young People*, 1988
- [ ] *Working It Out* [videorecording], 1990

GENERAL WEEDING GUIDELINES

300s
5 to 20 years

600s
5 to 15 years

Biography
5 to 10 years

Why Weed Women's Issues?

The topic of Women's Issues has been at the forefront for many years. Why revisit it now as a weeding topic? Because there are still many, many old titles in our collections. From titles like *All You Can Knit and Crochet for Women* to career books titled *What Can She Be?* they are still on the shelves! What message are we giving our girls?

Dewey Numbers to Check

Start in the 300 section: 305s (Social Groups), 320s (Political Science), 340s (Law), and 390s (Customs, Etiquette, Folklore). Then move to the 600s: 618s (Gynecology and Obstetrics) and 640s (Home and Family Management). In the 700s, look at 740s (Drawing and Decorative Arts) and the 796s (Athletic and Outdoor Sports and Games). Look at your biographies (especially the 920s) as well as the AV and professional collections.

Specific Criteria for Weeding

Carefully look at any books directed at "women's issues" and decide if the gender slant is justified in today's world. Although books on individual sports (track, basketball, etc.) may require a gender approach, does a book on investments? You might be better off weeding a gender-specific title and replacing it with a general-interest approach on some topics.

Topics that still justify a gender approach (some careers, lifestyle choices, etc.) should be evaluated to be sure that the content is encouraging to today's girls and not condescending or misleading. A valid message from twenty years ago could be more demoralizing than positive when read today.

Materials on gender-specific topics (breast cancer, pregnancy, etc.) that contain outdated information are also dangerous to have on the shelves and must be removed.

Tips for Replacing Titles

Update all those collective biographies of women achievers, both in topics and personalities.

Consider Weeding Titles Like These

- *1,001 Job Ideas for Today's Women: A Checklist Guide to the Job Market*, 1975
- *The Adolescent Girl in Conflict*, 1966
- *Affirmative Action for Women: A Practical Guide*, 1973
- *The Ambitious Woman's Guide to a Successful Career*, 1975
- *American Woman: New Opportunities* [filmstrip], 1976
- *American Women of Science*, 1955
- *American Women: The Changing Image*, 1962
- *Applied Mathematics for Girls*, 1963
- *A Better Figure for You through Easy Exercise and Diet*, 1965
- *Birth Control and Unmarried Young Women*, 1974
- *Bubble Bath and Hair Bow: A Little Girl's Guide to Grooming*, 1963
- *Careers for Women after Marriage and Children*, 1965
- *Charm: The Career Girl's Guide to Business and Personal Success*, 1971
- *Elegance: A Complete Guide for Every Woman Who Wants to Be Well and Properly Dressed on All Occasions*, 1964

- *Everything a Woman Needs to Know to Get Paid What She's Worth*, 1973
- *Few Are Chosen: American Women in Political Life Today*, 1968
- *For Women of All Ages: A Gynecologist's Guide to Modern Health Care*, 1979
- *The Future of Motherhood*, 1974
- *Future Perfect: A Guide to Personality and Popularity for the Junior Miss*, 1957
- *A Girl's Guide to Dating and Going Steady*, 1968
- *How to Get a Teen-Age Boy and What to Do with Him When You Get Him*, 1969
- *I Can Be Anything: Careers and Colleges for Young Women*, 1978
- *Legal Status of Women*, 1978
- *Modern Track and Field for Girls and Women*, 1973
- *A Woman's Money: How to Protect and Increase It in the Stock Market*, 1970

321.8
Democracy

GENERAL WEEDING GUIDELINES

300s
5 to 20 years

900s
5 to 15 years

Why Weed Democracy?

As political rhetoric continues to dominate the news and media coverage increases, students may be wondering about our system of government. A good library media collection will have materials that explain democracy (rule by the people) and the freedoms we cherish that allow for spirited debates and open elections. For students who go to the library book shelves (good for them!) as well as the Internet, make sure you have removed any outdated titles and replaced (or have plans to replace) them with current and forthcoming titles.

Dewey Numbers to Check

The current placement in Dewey for the topic of democracy is 321.8 (Democratic Government). But you may have titles in need of review throughout the 320s (Political Science). Also look in the 340s (Law) and the 350s (Public Administration) as well as the 973s (History, United States). You should also carefully review your reference and AV sections.

Specific Criteria for Weeding

The tradition and documents that define democracy in the United States are well established. Your collection will (or should) have titles on the Bill of Rights, the Constitution, the Declaration of Independence, and the Civil Rights Act of 1965. If some of your titles rival the age of those documents, weed them and replace with some of the new and attractive titles that will appeal to your readers and reinforce their understanding of democracy today.

You probably also have some titles that compare democracy to other forms of government in the world. Make sure that the "other world" cited is relevant today and does not center on dated systems such as communism in Russia.

As for filmstrips in your collection, remember that collection development in a library media center is not a democratic process! You know that filmstrips are an outdated format, so just discard them.

Tips for Replacing Titles

With democratic governments being established for the first time in many countries around the world, new titles are being published that reflect these developments. Take advantage of the news and provide interesting materials on the countries and emerging democracy.

Consider Weeding Titles Like These

- *American Democracy and Social Change,* 1938
- *American Democracy Debated: An Introduction to American Government,* 1978
- *American Democracy in Theory and Practice,* 1963
- *American Democracy in World Perspective,* 1967
- *American Democracy: Theory and Reality,* 1972
- *An American Dilemma: The Negro Problem and Modern Democracy,* 1962
- *The American Experience in Democracy* [filmstrip], 1974
- *The Challenge of American Democracy,* 1974
- *The Challenges to Democracy: Consensus and Extremism in American Politics,* 1965
- *Changing Governments and Changing Cultures: The World's March Towards Democracy,* 1932
- *Communism, Fascism, and Democracy: The Theoretical Foundations,* 1972
- *Current Issues in American Democracy,* 1975
- *The Deadlock of Democracy: Four-Party Politics in America,* 1963
- *Democracy: Ancient and Modern,* 1973
- *Democracy and Its Discontents: Reflections on Everyday America,* 1974
- *Democracy in a Revolutionary Era: The Political Order Today,* 1968
- *Diary of Democracy: The Story of Political Parties in America,* 1970
- *Education and Liberty: The Role of the Schools in a Modern Democracy,* 1953
- *The First Amendment and the Future of American Democracy,* 1976
- *Making the World Safe for Democracy,* 1975
- *Modern Arms and Free Men: A Discussion of the Role of Science in Preserving Democracy,* 1949
- *Speak Up for Democracy: What You Can Do—A Practical Plan of Action for Every American Citizen,* 1940
- *Symbols of Democracy* [filmstrip], 1975
- *Two Worlds in Conflict: Democracy vs. Communism,* 1965
- *Who Governs? Democracy and Power in an American City,* 1961

322
Terrorism

Why Weed Terrorism?

Since 2001 there has been great interest in the topic of terrorism, and the publishing industry has responded to that interest with a tremendous number of new titles. Now is the time to select the best of those new publications and to review the titles that you already have on your shelves. Before 2001, the last big publishing push on terrorism was in the 1970s, responding mainly to terrorism in the form of airplane hijackings. Those titles should now be weeded or updated to make room for the current terrorism titles.

Dewey Numbers to Check

GENERAL WEEDING GUIDELINES

300s
5 to 20 years

Any titles on terrorism will probably be found in your 300s (Social Sciences): general works in the 301–303s (Sociology and Anthropology, Social Interaction, and Social Processes), political groups in the 322s (Relation of the State to Organized Groups and Their Members), legal discussions in the 340s (Law), and prevention and defense in the 360s (Social Problems and Services). But you may find titles on this topic cataloged in other areas of the 300s or even in the 900s. Search by subject headings to find them all. Remember to check the reference and the AV collections also.

Specific Criteria for Weeding

Check any older titles on terrorism to see if they are based mostly on cases of terrorists using guns, bomb threats, or hijackings with the objective of obtaining money or the release of political prisoners. The nature of terrorism has changed along with the sources of political turmoil producing the terrorism. Also check to see if your older titles focus mainly on communism and the cold war as terrorist threats.

Methods of terrorist attacks have also changed over the years to include ever more lethal chemical and biological weapons. From crop-dusting planes to municipal water supplies, terrorist attack scenarios have multiplied and become much more sophisticated.

Past acts of terrorism (such as Pearl Harbor and the Munich Olympics) must remain documented for current students, but accounts should be updated and accurate from today's perspective.

Tips for Replacing Titles

Monitor the reviews on new titles on terrorism and purchase only the best to help your students understand this important and highly emotional topic. Be sure to have current atlases available also for students as they track world events.

Consider Weeding Titles Like These

- [ ] *Brothers in Blood: The International Terrorist Network*, 1977
- [ ] *Countering Palestinian Terrorism in Israel: Toward a Policy Analysis of Countermeasures*, 1980
- [ ] *Crusaders, Criminals, Crazies: Terror and Terrorism in Our Time*, 1976
- [ ] *Flying Scared: Why We Are Being Sky-jacked and How to Put a Stop to It*, 1972
- [ ] *Guerrilla Warfare and Terrorism*, 1977
- [ ] *International Terrorism and Political Crimes*, 1973
- [ ] *International Terrorism in the Contemporary World*, 1978
- [ ] *Language of Violence: The Blood Politics of Terrorism*, 1979
- [ ] *Living with Terrorism*, 1975
- [ ] *Political Terror in Communist Systems*, 1970
- [ ] *Political Terrorism*, 1974
- [ ] *Political Terrorism: The Threat and the Response*, 1976
- [ ] *The Struggle against Terrorism*, 1977

- [ ] *Studies in Nuclear Terrorism*, 1979
- [ ] *Terror and Resistance: A Study of Political Violence, with Case Studies of Some Primitive African Communities*, 1969
- [ ] *Terrorism* [filmstrip], 1979
- [ ] *Terrorism and Hostage Negotiations*, 1980
- [ ] *Terrorism: From Robespierre to Arafat*, 1976
- [ ] *Terrorism: Threat, Reality, Response*, 1979
- [ ] *Terrorism Worldwide: Is Anybody Safe?* [filmstrip], 1976
- [ ] *The Terrorist Mind*, 1974
- [ ] *The Terrorist: Their Weapons, Leaders and Tactics*, 1979
- [ ] *A Time of Terror: How Democratic Societies Respond to Revolutionary Violence*, 1978
- [ ] *The Ultimate Weapon: Terrorists and World Order*, 1978
- [ ] *Urban Terrorism: Theory, Practice and Response*, 1976

323
Civil Rights

**GENERAL WEEDING
GUIDELINES**

300s
5 to 20 years

Biography
5 to 10 years

Why Weed Civil Rights?

Demand for civil rights material remains solid over the years due to both school assignments and personal interest. However, the focus of civil rights continues to change. Does your collection represent only the civil rights focus of the 1960s and 1970s? Update and add to your collection for today's students.

Dewey Numbers to Check

Most of the titles on civil rights will be found in the 300s. Check the 305s (Social Groups) and the 323s (Civil and Political Rights). You will find titles on civil rights personalities in both the 920s (collective biographies) and the individual biography section. Remember to also check the reference section and the AV collection.

Specific Criteria for Weeding

During the 1960s and 1970s, "civil rights" focused specifically on racial equality. A combination of the publishing world's response and the availability of federal library funding resulted in strong collections in this area for K–12 school libraries. Civil rights materials based on racial equality are still relevant, but many of the players and issues have changed. And even if some of those players are still the same, the times and issues have changed. A student interested in the life of Coretta Scott King will not (or should not!) be satisfied with a biography written decades ago. Update all titles published on this era unless they are considered primary source materials.

The old formats in your AV collection should be updated with current content and formats. You can supplement while rebuilding by suggesting relevant websites.

Tips for Replacing Titles

The focus of civil rights has changed over the years to include concerns based on such issues as disabilities, sexual harassment and orientation, and treatment of various ethnic groups. Your collection should reflect these advances in perception.

Consider Weeding Titles Like These

- [ ] *Beyond Civil Rights: A New Day of Equality*, 1968
- [ ] *Black and White: A Study of U.S. Racial Attitudes Today*, 1967
- [ ] *Civil Rights: A Current Guide to the People, Organizations, and Events*, 1974
- [ ] *Civil Rights: The Constitution and the Courts*, 1967
- [ ] *Constitutional Rights of College Students: A Study in Case Law*, 1972
- [ ] *Coretta King: A Woman of Peace*, 1974
- [ ] *The First Book of American Negroes*, 1966
- [ ] *Freedom of the Press Today* [kit], 1969
- [ ] *The Indians Speak Out: Indian Civil Rights* [filmstrip], 1974
- [ ] *Justice in Everyday Life: The Way It Really Works*, 1974
- [ ] *Negro Protest Thought in the Twentieth Century*, 1966
- [ ] *The New Negro of the South: A Portrait of Movements and Leadership*, 1967
- [ ] *The People's Power: American Government and Politics Today*, 1973
- [ ] *Race and the News Media*, 1967

- [ ] *Racial Crisis in America: Leadership in Conflict*, 1964
- [ ] *The Rights of Servicemen: The Basic ACLU Guide to Servicemen's Constitutional Rights*, 1973
- [ ] *The Rights of Students: The Basic ACLU Guide to a Student's Constitutional Rights*, 1973
- [ ] *The Rights of Suspects*, 1973
- [ ] *The Rights of Teachers: The Basic ACLU Guide to a Teacher's Constitutional Rights*, 1973
- [ ] *The Rights of the Poor*, 1963
- [ ] *The Rights of Women: The Basic ACLU Guide to Women's Rights*, 1973
- [ ] *What Are Human Rights?* 1973
- [ ] *White Justice: Black Experience Today in America's Courtrooms*, 1971
- [ ] *Your Rights and Responsibilities as an American Citizen: A Civics Casebook*, 1967
- [ ] *Your Rights and What They Really Mean* [filmstrip], 1971

324
Presidential Elections

Why Weed Presidential Elections?

Sometimes you weed a section of your collection to prepare it for upcoming heavy use and interest. That will be every four years for presidential elections! Each election, review what you have and discard the outdated. Add the best of the current titles available, and be prepared to continue to add titles as they are released.

Dewey Numbers to Check

Most of your older titles on U.S. political parties and the election process will be in the 329s. This number is now unassigned and no longer used by Dewey. As of 1997, the number range for titles on these topics is the 324s (The Political Process). This would be a good time to review all your titles (published before 1997) in the 329s and decide if you want to weed any of them or relocate to the 324s. Be sure to check the reference and AV sections.

Specific Criteria for Weeding

Students who are following current political news and are interested in the political process will not want to pick up titles that were published twenty or thirty years ago! In some cases, the title has been updated and republished. If that title was useful in its time, consider replacing it with the updated version. Otherwise, discard it.

Look at any older titles to see if they are strictly limited to facts for specific past elections or if they also deal in general with other election issues labeled as current at the time of publication. Those issues may not match today's concerns about campaign finance reform, term limits, or post-2000 election changes. Discard any title that is misleading about today's issues. Also discard any item that by title alone implies currency or comprehensiveness.

Bias can be an issue with titles on this topic, especially in primary source material. Watch that you provide balance on controversial issues and personalities. Make sure your collection does not reflect personal opinion—yours or that of your predecessors.

Tips for Replacing Titles

Be sure you have some titles on the most recent presidential election. Then be prepared to replace some of the early titles rushed to press with later titles that may be better.

Consider Weeding Titles Like These

☐ *America Votes: What You Should Know about Elections Today,* 1976

☐ *By a Single Vote! One-Vote Decisions That Changed American History,* 1987

☐ *The Changing American Voter,* 1976

☐ *Choices and Echoes in Presidential Elections: Rational Man and Electoral Democracy,* 1978

☐ *Choosing the President: An Inside Guide to the Election,* 1988

☐ *The Coming to Power: Critical Presidential Elections in American History,* 1974

☐ *The Disappearing American Voter,* 1992

☐ *Electing the President,* 1995

☐ *The Election Book: People Pick a President,* 1992

☐ *The First Book of Elections,* 1972

☐ *The Great American Convention: A Political History of Presidential Elections,* 1976

☐ *A History of Presidential Elections,* 1957

☐ *How America Votes in Presidential Elections,* 1968

☐ *Interpreting Elections,* 1983

☐ *Media and Presidential Politics* [video-recording], 1988

☐ *The Other Candidates: Third Parties in Presidential Elections,* 1983

☐ *Presidential Elections since 1789,* 1975

☐ *Presidential Elections: Strategies of American Electoral Politics,* 1971

☐ *The Presidents of the United States: A History of the Presidents of the United States,* 1976

☐ *The Road to the White House: The Politics of Presidential Elections,* 1980

☐ *A Short History of Presidential Elections,* 1967

☐ *A Statistical History of the American Presidential Elections,* 1968

☐ *Third Parties in Presidential Elections,* 1974

325
Immigration

Why Weed Immigration?

Immigration has always been a factor in the American social and political scene. But the faces and the homelands of the immigrants continue to change over the years. Your collection should reflect all these changes and not represent a specific time frame.

Dewey Numbers to Check

Most of the titles on immigration will be found in the 300s. Check the 325s (International Migration and Colonization) and the 363s (Other Social Problems and Services). Also check the 304s (Factors Affecting Social Behavior) and the 305s (Social Groups). The fiction and biography sections will also have titles dealing with the personal side of immigration. Finally, check the reference and AV sections.

Specific Criteria for Weeding

There are many wonderful accounts in print of immigrants and their experiences coming to America in the 1800s and the early 1900s. The nationalities of those immigrants varied over those years, but most traced their roots to Europe. Since that time—and especially since 1965 when immigration laws were changed—a shift has occurred and most immigrants are now Asian, Latino, Arabic, and black. The faces have changed, but many of the emotional and physical struggles remain the same. Reading about those old struggles can reassure new immigrants, but the new stories need to be told also.

A strong collection on immigration will include both the old stories and the new. So what is there to weed? You should be looking at three main criteria: physical condition, bias, and format. But be careful not to discard any primary source materials that are not replaceable.

Tips for Replacing Titles

Many new titles on the market continue to tell the old stories as well as provide the new stories. New titles are more likely to be free of old biases and have formats that are more inviting. Be sure you have titles that tell the stories of your diverse community.

Consider Weeding Titles Like These

- *American Fever: The Story of American Immigration*, 1970
- *American Immigration Policies*, 1963
- *American Immigration Today: Pressures, Problem, Politics*, 1981
- *Becoming American: The Problems of Immigrants and Their Children*, 1970
- *Border Patrol: How U.S. Agents Protect Our Borders from Illegal Entry*, 1974
- *Building a Nation: The Story of Immigration* [filmstrip], 1983
- *Calculated Kindness: Refugees and America's Half-Open Door, 1945 to the Present*, 1986
- *Citizenship Education and Naturalization Information*, 1987
- *Coming to America: A History of Immigration and Ethnicity in American Life*, 1990
- *Dictionary of American Immigration History*, 1990
- *Eligibility for Entry to the United States of America*, 1967
- *Ethnic Americans: A History of Immigration and Assimilation*, 1982
- *For the People: U.S. Citizenship and Naturalization Information*, 1988

- *Friends or Strangers: The Impact of Immigrants on the U.S. Economy*, 1990
- *The Golden Door: International Migration, Mexico, and the United States*, 1981
- *The Immigrants* [filmstrip], 1974
- *Immigrants, Refugees, and U.S. Policy*, 1981
- *Immigration and Migration* [filmstrip], 1975
- *Immigration: Cultural Conflicts and Social Adjustments*, 1969
- *Immigration: Its Evils and Consequences*, 1969
- *Immigration Laws of the United States: A Guide to Admission to the United States*, 1953
- *Immigration Made Simple: An Easy-to-Read Guide to the U.S. Immigration Process*, 1990
- *Immigration: The Dream and the Reality* [filmstrip], 1970
- *Race and Ethnicity in Modern America*, 1974
- *They Came to America* [filmstrip], 1972
- *World Migration in Modern Times*, 1968

330
Personal Finance

**GENERAL WEEDING
GUIDELINES**

300s
5 to 20 years

Why Weed Personal Finance?

Personal finance has become more and more complicated over the years. Issues and procedures (such as filling out income tax forms) are more complex today, and the financial choices are more numerous (buying versus leasing a car, for example). And the stakes are very high for today's young people. Students are bombarded with credit card applications while still in high school. Your library media collection should contain personal finance materials that are current, attractive, and pertinent to your students' stage of life.

Dewey Numbers to Check

Most of your material on this topic will be in the 330s (Economics). Check the reference and AV collections also.

Specific Criteria for Weeding

Currency is the prime consideration in weeding your materials on personal finance. Just think how much the "numbers" have changed for you over the last twenty-some years! A book published even a decade ago will contain misleading figures for wages and living expenses. A student might be aware that the minimum wage rate has changed, but he or she might not have a clear understanding of changes in the cost of rent, utilities, and other necessities of life. When reviewing older titles, look for any numbers that you know are not relevant to the world of today.

In addition to content, consider the focus of titles in this area. Personal finance materials should relate to students at this stage of their lives. Although there may be some who are interested in building up a nest egg for retirement, the overwhelming majority are trying to figure out current problems, such as paying for a car or saving for college.

Tips for Replacing Titles

Because this topic is important to all students, even the reluctant reader, be sure to select solid titles that are also very readable and incorporate contemporary formatting, such as the "sidebar" style.

Consider Weeding Titles Like These

- *After the Crash: How to Survive and Prosper during the Depression of the 1980s*, 1980
- *The Battle for Financial Security: How to Invest in the Runaway 80s*, 1980
- *Consumer Credit and Money Management* [filmstrip], 1975
- *Consumer Economics Today and Tomorrow*, 1978
- *The Consumer in American Society: Personal and Family Finance*, 1974
- *Crisis Investing: Opportunities and Profits in the Coming Great Depression*, 1980
- *Dollars and Sense: The Teen-age Consumer's Guide*, 1975
- *The Economics of Being a Woman*, 1976
- *How to Get a Dollar's Value for a Dollar Spent*, 1964
- *How to Prosper during the Coming Bad Years*, 1979
- *How to Prosper during the Coming Good Years*, 1982
- *Living on a Shoestring: A Survival Guide for Coping with Finances, Furnishings, Receipts, Rents, and Roommates*, 1980
- *Long Range Planning* [filmstrip], 1976
- *Manage Your Money and Live Better: Get the Most from Your Dwindling Dollars*, 1971

- *Money and Kids: How to Earn It, Save It, and Spend It*, 1973
- *The Only Investment Guide You'll Ever Need*, 1979
- *The Practical Money Manager: A Guide and Workbook on How to Handle Your Money Profitably in Today's Economy*, 1974
- *The Small Investor's Handbook for Long-Term Security or Quick Profit*, 1969
- *Squeeze It Till the Eagle Grins: How to Spend, Save and Enjoy Your Money*, 1972
- *Using a Charge Account* [sound recording], 1978
- *Using a Checking Account* [filmstrip], 1978
- *Using Credit and Banking Services and Understanding Income Tax*, 1980
- *Welcome to the Real World: A Guide to Making Your First Personal, Financial, and Career Decisions*, 1979
- *Your Money and Your Life: How to Plan Your Long-Range Financial Security*, 1979
- *Your Money and What to Do with It: A Primer for the Inexperienced in the Handling, Conserving, and Investment of Funds*, 1960

331
Careers

Why Weed Careers?

Career guidance titles are some of the most time-sensitive materials in a media center! When students are seeking career information, they need the most current information in addition to authoritative projections on trends and employment opportunities. Even a few years can make a big difference in specific career areas. Outdated career materials may mislead your students when they are considering career choices.

Dewey Numbers to Check

Review the 331s (Labor Economics) and 371s (Schools and Their Activities) for general career information. However, titles on careers in specific vocations are generally classed with those specific subject areas. Check the reference and AV sections as well as any "career corner" collections.

Specific Criteria for Weeding

In reviewing career information, watch for bias as well as generally outdated and wrong information. Look for bias in gender, race, and ethnic group in illustrations or photographs of people in specific careers. Are all nurses women and all computer programmers men? Students must "see themselves" in a career as well as read about it. Although some careers have undergone drastic changes over the years, even careers that seem relatively static (such as library careers) have experienced significant changes in educational preparation and job responsibilities—as you know!

Because many career titles are shelved with specific subject areas, you can review current titles on the subject and compare them to the career titles sitting on the shelf nearby. For example, you will find that a career book on working with computers is outdated even if it is only five years old.

Tips for Replacing Titles

Although elementary school collections should have a well-balanced assortment of all general career areas, secondary collections can focus more on what is hot now. Check with guidance counselors and pay attention to what the publishing industry has recognized as in demand.

Consider Weeding Titles Like These

- *100 Careers: How to Pick the One That's Best for You*, 1977
- *The Airline Cabin Attendant* [filmstrip], 1973
- *The Ambitious Woman's Guide to a Successful Career*, 1975
- *Career Diplomat: A Career in the Foreign Service of the United States*, 1964
- *A Career for Tomorrow* [filmstrip], 1976
- *Career Planning for High School Students*, 1953
- *Careers and Opportunities in Astronautics*, 1962
- *Careers and Opportunities in the Medical Sciences*, 1971
- *Careers in Computing: A TRS-80 Computer Program* [filmstrip], 1982
- *Careers Today*, 1977
- *Challenging Careers in the Library World*, 1970
- *Charm: The Career Girl's Guide to Business and Personal Success*, 1964
- *Choices for Tomorrow*, 1978
- *Disease Detectives: Your Career in Medical Research*, 1959
- *Exciting Careers for Home Economists*, 1967
- *Executive Careers for Women*, 1961
- *Forestry and Its Career Opportunities*, 1952
- *Guide to Career Information: A Bibliography of Recent Occupational Literature*, 1957
- *Here Is Your Career: Airline Pilot*, 1978
- *Larry the Letter Carrier* [filmstrip], 1974
- *Welcome to the Real World: A Guide to Making Your First Personal, Financial, and Career Decisions*, 1979
- *Women's Place: Options and Limits in Professional Careers*, 1970
- *World of Work: Is a Career in Atomic Energy for You?* [videorecording], 1974
- *Your Career in Teaching*, 1967

332
The Stock Market

Why Weed the Stock Market?

Students of all ages are hearing, seeing, and reading news about the stock market, investments, and the economy: on TV, in newspapers and magazines, and at the family dinner table. They may have unemployed relatives or be facing canceled vacations and changes to family budgets. Students may look for answers or reassurance from your collection.

Dewey Numbers to Check

The 332s (Financial Economics) is where you will find titles on the stock market and investments. Also check reference and the AV collection.

Specific Criteria for Weeding

Many of the popular titles on this topic are written from the "how to" point of view. But we all know that the "how to" changes along with the market. What might be a popular approach to stocks and investments in a boom market would not be recommended for other times. Review your titles to see if they are giving good information for *all* times and not just for the bull or bear market "current at the time of publication." Be especially careful of keeping titles that are older but imply currency in the title or the approach.

Titles that have a historical perspective are also important to the collection, but that perspective is better from a current vantage point, unless the items are primary source materials (not often found on this topic at the K–12 level). As with all topics, format is important. Replace older titles (and those filmstrips) with newer publications.

Tips for Replacing Titles

Since the publishing world can't predict stock market conditions, you may have to supplement with some online resources until solid titles are released.

Consider Weeding Titles Like These

- [ ] *100 to 1 in the Stock Market: A Distinguished Security Analyst Tells How to Make More of Your Investment Opportunities,* 1972

- [ ] *The Common Sense Way to Stock Market Profits,* 1968

- [ ] *Everybody's Guide to the Stock Market,* 1959

- [ ] *Gaining on the Market: Your Complete Guide to Investment Strategy, Stocks, Bonds, Options, Mutual Funds, and Gold,* 1988

- [ ] *The Great Bull Market: Wall Street in the 1920s,* 1968

- [ ] *Handbook of the Stock Market: A Guide to the Language of the Investment World,* 1970

- [ ] *How to Make the Stock Market Make Money for You,* 1966

- [ ] *How Wall Street Doubles My Money Every Three Years: The No-Nonsense Guide to Steady Stock Market Profits,* 1969

- [ ] *Intelligent Investing: Profit-Making Moves in the Stock Market,* 1971

- [ ] *Investing in Securities: A Handbook for Today's Market,* 1975

- [ ] *Investment Opportunities for the Mid 1980's: Wealth-Building Strategies in the Stock Market, Gold, Silver, Diamonds,* 1985

- [ ] *The Low-High Theory of Investment: How to Make Money in the Stock Market and Keep It,* 1968

- [ ] *Odds-on Investing: Survival and Success in the New Stock Market,* 1978

- [ ] *Risk and Opportunity: A New Approach to Stock Market Profits,* 1974

- [ ] *The Roaring '80s on Wall Street: How to Make a Killing in the Coming Stock Market Boom,* 1981

- [ ] *The Smart Money: How to Invest in the Stock Market Like an Insider,* 1972

- [ ] *The Stock Market* [filmstrip], 1979

- [ ] *The Stock Market and "Me": An Independent Approach to Wall Street,* 1974

- [ ] *The Stock Market Indicators, as a Guide to Market Timing,* 1968

- [ ] *The Stock Market Investment Club Handbook: How to Organize, Maintain, and Profit from an Investment Club,* 1971

- [ ] *Stock Market Profits and Higher Income for You,* 1975

- [ ] *Stock Market Scams, Swindles, and Scoundrels: How to Recognize and Avoid Them,* 1972

- [ ] *Teenagers' Guide to the Stock Market and What Their Parents Ought to Know,* 1965

- [ ] *Understanding the Stock Market: A Guide for Young Investors,* 1968

- [ ] *The Young Investor's Guide to the Stock Market,* 1972

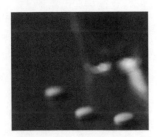

360
Drug and Alcohol Education

**GENERAL WEEDING
GUIDELINES**

300s
5 to 20 years

600s
5 to 15 years

Why Weed Drug and Alcohol Education?

There's no question that information on drug and alcohol education is critically needed in all our schools. But even more critical is the need for current and relevant information. Students tend to turn to their peers instead of adults for real-world information on drugs and alcohol—a tendency reinforced by outdated and/or inaccurate information in library collections.

Dewey Numbers to Check

Most materials will be found in two areas: the 360s (Social Problems and Services) on drug dependencies and trafficking, and the 613.8s (Personal Health and Safety—Drug Abuse) on messages to avoid addictions. You may also have materials in the 306s (Culture and Institutions) on the subculture of substance abuse, and in the 616s (Diseases) on the medical aspects. Also check the reference, professional, and AV collections.

Specific Criteria for Weeding

Review content, accuracy, and presentation for this topic. Substances that are used and abused change over the years—what was hot and available in years past may not be on the streets now. And the drugs that pose the most dangers to students today may be new to the streets and missing from old titles. Accuracy is also critical. Marijuana is cheaper and more readily available than ever before. The sources and potency of heroin have changed dramatically, so old information may now be deadly information. Even moderate alcohol use is now believed to carry dangers that were not known several years ago. The presentation of information can make all the difference in the way the information is received. If an item looks dated, students probably won't take it off the shelf unless required to by an assignment. Either way, it is bad news—dangerous news—for students.

This is a topic where the AV collection may be even more important than the print. Most students receive drug and alcohol information in school via an AV presentation instead of through personal instruction or reading on their own. Review carefully and discard old formats and dated information.

Tips for Replacing Titles

Personal narratives, old and new, can be useful in reinforcing the dangers of drug and alcohol abuse. Update the biography and AV collections with new titles.

Consider Weeding Titles Like These

- [ ] *Adolescents, Alcohol, and Drugs: A Practical Guide for Those Who Work with Young People*, 1988
- [ ] *Alcohol and Drugs: Making the Right Decision* [videorecording], 1990
- [ ] *Alcohol and Social Responsibility: A New Educational Approach*, 1949
- [ ] *Alcohol: Crisis for the Unborn* [videorecording], 1977
- [ ] *The Alcohol Problem*, 1948
- [ ] *Alcohol, Tobacco, and Drugs: Their Use and Abuse*, 1977
- [ ] *Back on the Streets: A Documentary on Teen Drug and Alcohol Abuse* [videorecording], 1986
- [ ] *Basic Information on Alcohol*, 1964
- [ ] *The College Drug Scene*, 1968
- [ ] *Drinking among Teen-agers: A Sociological Interpretation of Alcohol Use by High School Students*, 1964
- [ ] *Drug Abuse: Escape to Nowhere; A Guide for Educators*, 1967
- [ ] *Drug Abuse: Glue-Sniffing and Pills, Marijuana and LSD* [filmstrip], 1968

- [ ] *Drug Abuse: Pot and Thrill Pills*, 1967
- [ ] *Drug Addiction in Youth*, 1965
- [ ] *Drug Addiction: Physiological, Psychological, and Sociological Aspects*, 1958
- [ ] *Drugs in Our Society (Narcotics): Critical Areas of Health* [filmstrip], 1965
- [ ] *Drugs in Today's World* [filmstrip], 1971
- [ ] *Facts about Drugs, Alcohol, and Tobacco* [filmstrip], 1972
- [ ] *Marijuana: Facts, Myths and Decisions* [videorecording], 1981
- [ ] *Narcotics and the Law: A Critique of the American Experiment in Narcotic Drug Control*, 1967
- [ ] *Stand Up for Yourself: Peer Pressure and Drugs* [videorecording], 1986
- [ ] *Teaching about Alcohol*, 1964
- [ ] *Teen-Age Drinking*, 1968
- [ ] *Young People and Drinking: The Use and Abuse of the Beverage Alcohol*, 1963

362.4
Disabilities

GENERAL WEEDING GUIDELINES

100s
5 to 10 years

300s
5 to 20 years

600s
5 to 15 years

Why Weed Disabilities?

Perhaps because of more accurate tests and diagnoses, more students with special needs are in all our classrooms and library media centers today. Library media collections should provide updated titles that promote understanding and acceptance of these students.

Dewey Numbers to Check

You will have to check several areas to find all the materials on disabilities and people with various disabilities: the 155.9s (Environmental Psychology), 305.9s (Occupational and Miscellaneous Groups), 362.4s (Problems of and Services to People with Physical Disabilities), 371.9s (Special Education), and 649.8s (Home Care of Persons with Disabilities and Illnesses). Also review your reference and AV collections.

Specific Criteria for Weeding

The diagnosis and identification of disabilities and disorders have evolved over recent years. For example, attention deficit hyperactivity disorder (ADHD) is increasingly diagnosed. Asperger's syndrome, a condition related to autism, is now an identified condition. Older titles do not have this information; new titles should. Use keywords like these to quickly check the currency of titles in your collection.

In 1990 the Individuals with Disabilities Education Act and the Americans with Disabilities Act were passed, and any title published before that year addressing social services for people with disabilities is now outdated. Discard and replace such items.

Tips for Replacing Titles

More titles on disabilities are being marketed today to help students with acceptance and tolerance. Some of these titles are showing up in the fiction market also. Check your older titles (especially AV) to make sure the message and sensitivities are right. Then add some of the new titles from today's market. Remember that not all disabilities are visible.

Consider Weeding Titles Like These

- [ ] *Access: The Guide to a Better Life for Disabled Americans*, 1978
- [ ] *Art Projects for the Mentally Retarded Child*, 1976
- [ ] *Auditory Disorders in Children*, 1970
- [ ] *Autism: Diagnosis, Current Research, and Management*, 1976
- [ ] *Basic Lessons for Retarded Children*, 1965
- [ ] *Blindness: What It Is, What It Does, and How to Live with It*, 1961
- [ ] *Caring for Your Disabled Child*, 1965
- [ ] *Consumer's Guide to Mental Health Services*, 1980
- [ ] *Crafts for Retarded: Through Their Hands They Shall Learn*, 1964
- [ ] *Deaf Children at Home and School*, 1967
- [ ] *Disabled Workers in the Labor Market*, 1964
- [ ] *Down's Syndrome (Mongolism): Research, Prevention, and Management*, 1975
- [ ] *Employment for the Handicapped: A Guide for the Disabled, Their Families, and Their Counselors*, 1967
- [ ] *The Epilepsy Fact Book*, 1977
- [ ] *Every Kid Is Special* [filmstrip], 1977
- [ ] *A Handbook of Emotional Illness and Treatment: A Contemporary Guide with Case Histories*, 1962
- [ ] *Handbook of Mental Retardation Syndromes*, 1975
- [ ] *Legal Aspects of Educating the Developmentally Disabled*, 1975
- [ ] *The Link between Learning Disabilities and Juvenile Delinquency: Current Theory and Knowledge*, 1976
- [ ] *Meet Scott: He's a Special Person*, 1978
- [ ] *Recreation for Retarded Teenagers and Young Adults*, 1968
- [ ] *Stress and Distress: A Psychiatrist's Guide to Modern Living*, 1971
- [ ] *Teaching Individuals with Physical and Multiple Disabilities*, 1976
- [ ] *When Children Need Help: An Up-to-Date Handbook of Guidance for Parents of Children Who Have Been Diagnosed as Brain-Injured, Mentally Retarded, Cerebral Palsied, Learning Disabled, or as a Slow Learner*, 1972
- [ ] *When Mental Illness Strikes Your Family*, 1951

363.2
Forensic Science

Why Weed Forensic Science?

Most library media specialists would love to increase their students' nonfiction leisure reading habits. One sure way to do this is to provide nonfiction reading materials on current subjects of high interest, such as forensic science. But do you have any titles on this topic? If so, how current are they? Perry Mason era? Quincy era? Or CSI-ready?

Dewey Numbers to Check

Look in the 363.2s (Police Services) and 364s (Criminology) for titles on this topic. Also look in the 614–615s (Forensic Medicine—Pharmacology) for titles on medical forensics and toxicology. The reference section probably won't have any titles, but the AV collection might have one or two.

Specific Criteria for Weeding

Criteria for weeding this section include evaluating titles according to content and currency. Some forensic science techniques have been used and accepted for decades. Fingerprinting (or dactylography) was first used in England in the early 1900s for a criminal prosecution, and the technique is still widely used and respected. Titles that describe historical crime detection using tools of the day are still valuable to today's readers.

Recently developed detection techniques range from cyberforensics to forensic meteorology. Your students are probably very much aware of many of these new techniques from having logged many hours watching today's popular crime detection TV shows and movies. Because of this, you need to consider weeding (or updating) any title that even suggests a comprehensive look at the use of forensic science now.

Tips for Replacing Titles

As students consider their interest in forensic sciences, look for titles on career opportunities in this field. Chemistry labs and criminal justice programs are hot on college campuses now, so watch for good career guidance titles.

Consider Weeding Titles Like These

- [ ] *Ballistic Science for the Law Enforcement Officer*, 1977
- [ ] *Beyond the Crime Lab: The New Science of Investigation*, 1990
- [ ] *Cause of Death: The Story of Forensic Science*, 1980
- [ ] *Chemistry and Crime: From Sherlock Holmes to Today's Courtroom*, 1983
- [ ] *Crime and Science: The New Frontier in Criminology*, 1967
- [ ] *Crime Labs: The Science of Forensic Medicine*, 1979
- [ ] *Crime Scene Search and Physical Evidence Handbook*, 1974
- [ ] *Criminal Investigation: Basic Perspectives*, 1970
- [ ] *Criminalistics: An Introduction to Forensic Science*, 1977
- [ ] *Criminalistics: Theory and Practice*, 1980
- [ ] *Detective Work: A Study of Criminal Investigations*, 1977
- [ ] *Forensic Biology for the Law Enforcement Officer*, 1974
- [ ] *Forensic Geology: Earth Sciences and Criminal Investigation*, 1975

- [ ] *Forensic Science: An Introduction to Criminalistics*, 1983
- [ ] *Forensic Toxicology for the Law Enforcement Officer*, 1980
- [ ] *Handbook for Dental Identification: Techniques in Forensic Dentistry*, 1973
- [ ] *Handbook of Forensic Science*, 1975
- [ ] *Inside the Crime Lab*, 1974
- [ ] *Introduction to Forensic Sciences*, 1980
- [ ] *An Introduction to Modern Criminal Investigation: With Basic Laboratory Techniques*, 1978
- [ ] *Murder, Suicide, or Accident: The Forensic Pathologist at Work*, 1971
- [ ] *The Police Lab at Work*, 1967
- [ ] *Science Catches the Criminal*, 1975
- [ ] *The Science of Murder* [videorecording], 1988
- [ ] *Science Stalks the Criminal* [videorecording], 1989

370
Education

Why Weed Education?

What could be more professional than a current and appropriate collection on education? What is more unprofessional than an outdated and inaccurate collection of education titles? Of all the collections in your library media center, the professional collection on education should be weeded with a vengeance.

Dewey Numbers to Check

Education titles most often are grouped in a small, separate collection area—often called the Professional Collection. Most titles will be classed in the 370s (Education), but some will be classed with the various subject areas.

Specific Criteria for Weeding

Do you remember the 1960s? As an educator? As a child? As ancient history? In any case, you will no doubt agree that K–12 education and the approach to students have changed dramatically in the past few decades. However, many K–12 library media center professional collections are still based on publications from the 1960s. If your professional collection and education titles are still living in the 1960s, you need to both weed and add new titles. Methods of teaching as well as student discipline have changed, as has legal recourse. Approaches to students with learning disabilities or with social or medical problems have evolved.

Students (and young teachers!) are much more sophisticated today. Activity and crafts books from past generations may not have much appeal to the student accustomed to today's visual arts. Likewise, a new teacher may be only mildly amused by finding books on bulletin boards that deal with just pushpins and flannel!

Tips for Replacing Titles

Teaching-method materials that target specific subject areas afford you an ideal opportunity to collaborate with teachers on the rebuilding as well as the weeding of those areas. Be sure you have titles to meet the needs of your teachers who are trying to keep up to date professionally by attending workshops, taking courses, or reading about the latest strategies and methods.

Consider Weeding Titles Like These

- [ ] *Alcohol-Narcotics Education: A Handbook for Teachers*, 1967
- [ ] *Better Teaching in Secondary Schools*, 1964
- [ ] *Breakthrough in Teacher Education*, 1968
- [ ] *The Changing Curriculum: Science*, 1966
- [ ] *The Complexities of an Urban Classroom*, 1968
- [ ] *The Courts and the Public Schools*, 1955
- [ ] *Current Trends in Science Education*, 1966
- [ ] *Developing Vocational Instruction*, 1967
- [ ] *Discipline in Education* [filmstrip], 1964
- [ ] *English Today and Tomorrow: A Guide for Teachers of English*, 1964
- [ ] *Identifying Children with Special Needs*, 1955
- [ ] *Improving the Secondary-School Curriculum: A Guide to Effective Curriculum Planning*, 1970
- [ ] *Issues in American Education: Commentary on the Current Scene*, 1970
- [ ] *Learning Disabilities: Educational Principles and Practices*, 1967
- [ ] *Let Them Be Themselves: Language Arts Enrichment for Disadvantaged Children in Elementary Schools*, 1969
- [ ] *The Mentally Retarded Child in the Classroom*, 1965
- [ ] *Modern Elementary Curriculum*, 1966
- [ ] *New Conceptions of Vocational and Technical Education*, 1967
- [ ] *New Trends in the Schools*, 1967
- [ ] *Preparation and Use of Audio-Visual Aids*, 1955
- [ ] *Reforming American Education: The Innovative Approach to Improving Our Schools and Colleges*, 1969
- [ ] *Research for Tomorrow's Schools: Disciplined Inquiry for Education*, 1969
- [ ] *The Teachers' Library: How to Organize It and What to Include*, 1968
- [ ] *Teaching in a Modern Secondary School*, 1965
- [ ] *Teaching the Disadvantaged: New Curriculum Approaches*, 1966
- [ ] *The Years Before School: Guiding Preschool*, 1970
- [ ] *Your Future in Elementary School Teaching*, 1961

380
Transportation

Why Weed Transportation?

All students deal with the issue of transportation every day. Transportation schedules and methods sometimes determine the framework of their days. In addition to logistics, there is a natural interest in the various forms of transportation. The curiosity is there from their first words to their first bikes, first cars, and first travels. Your collection should encourage that interest and help students learn about this vital part of society and life today.

Dewey Numbers to Check

Transportation is a fairly easy topic to check since most of the titles will be found in the 380s (Commerce, Communications, Transportation) and 620s (Engineering and Allied Operations). Also check the reference and AV collections.

Specific Criteria for Weeding

Because students actually *use* transportation every day, currency is a prime consideration. Do the cars, buses, and airplanes in your books look like those your students see and use on a regular basis? Students will know and discount the outdated. There may be some interest in classic or older models, but most of your titles should be as contemporary as the transportation in your community.

Depictions of both vehicles and people are important. Look for gender and ethnic balance in illustrations. Some older titles may discuss personal transportation safety in a light much different from today's world of congestion and road rage. Air travel is a common means of transportation for some students. Books on airports and airplanes should reflect today's conditions as well as yesterday's.

Tips for Replacing Titles

Try to include some titles that explore modern transportation methods such as bullet trains or light rail. Although such means of transport might be used only in a few cosmopolitan areas today, they are projected to be available in many communities in the future.

Consider Weeding Titles Like These

- [ ] *Airliners from 1919 to the Present Day*, 1966
- [ ] *America Travels: The Story of a Hundred Years of Travel in America*, 1933
- [ ] *Big City Transportation*, 1954
- [ ] *The Boys' Book of Buses of the World*, 1961
- [ ] *Busy Waterways: The Story of America's Inland Water Transportation*, 1964
- [ ] *Cave Man to Space Man: Picture-History of Transportation*, 1961
- [ ] *A History of Land Transportation*, 1963
- [ ] *Let's Go to a Truck Terminal*, 1964
- [ ] *Megalopolis Unbound: The Supercity and Transportation of Tomorrow*, 1966
- [ ] *Moving Around the World: Travel by Road and Rail*, 1968
- [ ] *The New World of Helicopters*, 1967
- [ ] *A Picture History of U.S. Transportation on Rails, Roads, and Rivers*, 1958
- [ ] *Popular Mechanics' Picture History of American Transportation*, 1952

- [ ] *The Story of American Railroads*, 1967
- [ ] *This Is an Airport*, 1967
- [ ] *Transportation by Bus* [filmstrip], 1968
- [ ] *Transportation in the World of the Future*, 1968
- [ ] *Transportation in Today's World*, 1965
- [ ] *Transportation of Tomorrow*, 1968
- [ ] *What You'd See at the Airport* [filmstrip], 1968
- [ ] *What You'd See at the Harbor* [filmstrip], 1968
- [ ] *What You'd See at the Railroad Terminal* [filmstrip], 1968
- [ ] *Wings, Wheels, and Motors: A Book about How We Travel*, 1958
- [ ] *World of Tomorrow: Transport on Earth*, 1981
- [ ] *Your Career in Transportation*, 1966

392
Dating and Courtship

GENERAL WEEDING GUIDELINES

300s
5 to 20 years

600s
5 to 15 years

Why Weed Dating and Courtship?

The age-old rite of dating with its images of hearts and flowers! Some things never change—or do they? Although older titles on dating debated "going steady," today's publications may include a discussion of date rape and abuse, topics that unfortunately reflect a more honest look at some relationships. The dating scene has changed; so should your collection.

Dewey Numbers to Check

Titles on dating and courtship will be scattered across the 100s, 300s, and 600s. Start with the 306s (Culture and Institutions), 362.8s (for older titles on rape and dating violence; the current classification is 613.8), and the 392s (Customs of Life Cycle and Domestic Life). Move on to the 646.7s (Management of Personal and Family Life) and then to the 177s (Ethics of Social Relations). Do a subject search to find titles hiding in other classifications as well as fiction. The AV collection should be reviewed also.

Specific Criteria for Weeding

The dating scene of just twenty years ago was much different from that of today. When checking the content of titles on dating, focus on both what is included and what is missing. Any discussion of sexual involvement must be up to date with current dangers. Dating today can include social drugs that were unheard of just a few years ago. Types of dates also have changed over the years—from drive-in movies then to all-night raves now. Violence in relationships may not have been discussed in older books, but it must be now.

Gender slant should also be considered. Older titles may give the impression that a girl's objective must be to "find a man and get married" and not include an element of choice.

Tips for Replacing Titles

The heartache from a broken romance remains the same over the years, but look for contemporary titles (in both fiction and nonfiction) in order to appeal to today's youth.

Consider Weeding Titles Like These

- *The American Girl Book of First Dates*, 1963
- *The Art of Dating*, 1967
- *The Book of Dating: A Complete Guide to Dating and Social Conduct for Boys and Girls*, 1965
- *Boyfriends: Getting Them, Keeping Them, Living Without Them*, 1990
- *Boys Talk About Girls, Girls Talk About Boys*, 1981
- *Choosing a Marriage Partner*, 1979
- *Dating and Sex: Values, Attitudes, and Behavior* [filmstrip], 1979
- *The Dating Book: A Guide to the Social Scene*, 1983
- *Dating in the 90s: Feeling Good about Yourself* [videorecording], 1990
- *Dating Problems of Older Teens* [filmstrip], 1969
- *Dating, Sex, and Trouble* [videorecording], 1990
- *Everything You Need to Know about Date Rape*, 1989
- *A Fine Romance: The Passage of Courtship from Meeting to Marriage*, 1988
- *A Girl's Guide to Dating and Going Steady*, 1968
- *His and Hers: Dating Manners*, 1970
- *How Can You Tell if You're Really in Love* [filmstrip], 1979
- *The Seventeen Book of Answers to What Your Parents Don't Talk About and Your Best Friends Can't Tell You*, 1972
- *She-Manners*, 1970
- *The Teen Guide to Dating*, 1980
- *Teens Ask Questions about Family, Friends, and Dating*, 1972
- *The Truth about What Women Want in Men*, 1980
- *Two in a Crowd: How to Find Romance without Losing Your Friends*, 1985
- *Values for Dating* [filmstrip], 1974
- *We've Only Just Begun: A Guide to Successful Courtship*, 1982
- *Your Dating Days: Looking Forward to Successful Marriage*, 1971

394
Holidays

GENERAL WEEDING GUIDELINES

300s
5 to 20 years

700s
5 to 10 years

Why Weed Holidays?

Holiday materials in a library media collection are often thought of as immune from weeding. After all, holidays are all about traditions. But there are many different holiday traditions represented in our schools today. Also, remember that young people approach holidays with more than just anticipation. They are learning about holiday customs as well as dealing with holiday stress. Be sure that your collection of holiday titles teaches the traditional holiday stories in a way that is not detrimental to today's child—regardless of his or her gender, religion, race, or family setting.

Dewey Numbers to Check

See the 394.26s (Holidays) for general information. Craft books on holiday decorations will be found in the 745s (Decorative Arts). Find holiday poetry in the 811s (American Poetry in English) and plays in the 812s (American Drama in English). Check the reference and AV sections as well as fiction.

Specific Criteria for Weeding

Since holiday titles are a subject area that is often neglected in general weeding, first look for titles that are just physically too old, dirty, tattered, or smelly to leave in the collection! If the title is still valuable but in poor condition, replace it with a new edition or a comparable title.

Look at the remaining titles in the collection to check other criteria. First, consider the ethnic diversity of your collection. Does it include the cultures and backgrounds of all your students or just a portion of them? The collection should show the same diversity as your students—and should support their own traditions as well as teach other students about those traditions. Next, consider gender sensitivity. Be on the lookout for titles and illustrations in which only little girls are baking cookies with their mothers while the little boys are hanging decorations with their fathers. Finally, remember that not all children are cocooned in the nuclear families represented in many of the older titles.

Tips for Replacing Titles

From the many holiday titles that are published each year, select ones that support traditional values but also recognize the diversity in today's world.

Consider Weeding Titles Like These

- [ ] *The American Christmas: A Study in National Culture*, 1954
- [ ] *Anniversaries and Holidays: A Calendar of Days and How to Observe Them*, 1944
- [ ] *Bulletin Boards for Holidays and Seasons*, 1958
- [ ] *Celebrating Christmas around the World*, 1962
- [ ] *Celebrations for Special Occasions: Mother's Day, Music Week, Graduation Day, Father's Day, Halloween, Book Week*, 1940
- [ ] *Christmas: A Book of Stories Old and New*, 1950
- [ ] *Christmas All Year 'Round: Twenty-five Christmas Stories from the American Girl*, 1952
- [ ] *A Christmas Book: An Anthology for Moderns*, 1928
- [ ] *Christmas Customs around the World*, 1959
- [ ] *Christmas Everywhere: A Book of Christmas Customs of Many Lands*, 1936
- [ ] *Christmas in Many Lands* [filmstrip], 1952
- [ ] *Christmas Lighting and Decorating: Outdoors and Indoors*, 1954
- [ ] *Christmas with Our World Neighbors* [filmstrip], 1957

- [ ] *The Giant Halloween Book: Recitations, Dialogues, Plays, Readings, Pantomines, Song and Dance Skits, Action Songs, Dances, Marches for All Ages*, 1934
- [ ] *Holiday Cards for You to Make*, 1940
- [ ] *Holiday Craft and Fun: Party-Craft for Holidays, Including Invitations, Favors, Decorations and Centerpieces, Party Hats, Costumes and Games Easily Made at Home*, 1950
- [ ] *Holiday Plays for Teenagers: A Collection of One-Act, Royalty-Free Plays for Important Occasions*, 1952
- [ ] *Let's Celebrate Christmas: Parties, Plays, Legends, Carols, Poetry, Stories*, 1950
- [ ] *Modern Religious Dramas*, 1928
- [ ] *Month-by-Month Decorations*, 1958
- [ ] *A New Look at Christmas Decorations*, 1957
- [ ] *New Plays for Every Day the Schools Celebrate*, 1936
- [ ] *Plays for Our American Holidays*, 1928
- [ ] *The Southern Christmas Book: The Full Story from Earliest Times to the Present*, 1958

398
Folktales

GENERAL WEEDING GUIDELINES

300s
5 to 20 years

700s
5 to 10 years

Weed older Version & Unattractive titles

Why Weed Folktales?

Folktales by their very nature do not become obsolete. But folktales must still be weeded on the basis of the retelling of those tales. Older versions may be unacceptable to the modern reader due to biases or appearance. Weeding unattractive titles and then adding new titles will make the folktales section more appealing to students.

Dewey Numbers to Check

Folklore and folktales will usually be found in the 398s (Folklore). But there may be some in the 900s with travel and the history of individual countries or in the 745s (Decorative Arts). Also check the reference and AV sections.

Specific Criteria for Weeding

Biased pt. of View
Illustration World wide?
Appearance
Text Font

Review the folktales section to identify titles with text or illustrations displaying a biased point of view. Look for ethnic, religious, and gender biases. Consider whether specific titles (or even the collection as a whole) contribute to a wider view of the world or represent only the Western world.

Consider also the illustrations and overall appearance of each work. Look for older works with very little eye appeal for the reader. Weed titles with illustrations that are not appealing and/or supportive of the text. Also consider weeding any title with text that isn't readable by the students in your school because of font size, vocabulary level, and number of words per page.

Tips for Replacing Titles

Goal – Increase Global awareness

Adding new folktales to a collection is a great opportunity to increase students' global awareness. Students can better understand countries and cultures in the news today by studying their folktales and customs.

Consider Weeding Titles Like These

- *African Folktales* [filmstrip], 1970
- *American Negro Folktales*, 1967
- *Arab Folktales*, 1986
- *Black Folktales*, 1969
- *The Boy Who Could Do Anything and Other Mexican Folktales*, 1942
- *The Boy Who Found the Light: Eskimos Folktales*, 1990
- *Burmese and Thai Fairy Tales*, 1967
- *The Burro Benedicto and Other Folktales and Legends of Mexico*, 1960
- *Complete Book of Indian Crafts and Lore*, 1954
- *The Cow-Tail Switch and Other West African Stories*, 1947
- *Damian and the Dragon: Modern Greek Folktales*, 1965
- *The Eskimo Storyteller: Folktales from Noatak, Alaska*, 1975
- *The Fire on the Mountain and Other Ethiopian Stories*, 1950
- *The Five Chinese Brothers*, 1938
- *Gone Is Gone; or, The Story of a Man Who Wanted to Do Housework*, 1935

- *Indian Adventure Trails: Tales of Trails and Tipis, Ponies and Paddles, Warpaths and Warriors*, 1953
- *Pawnee Hero Stories and Folktales: With Notes on the Origin, Customs, and Character of the Pawnee People*, 1961
- *Red Man, White Man: Legends, Tales and True Accounts of the American Indians*, 1957
- *Stories from Japan*, 1960
- *Stories from Old Russia*, 1964
- *Three Gay Tales from Grimm*, 1943
- *Told by Uncle Remus: New Stories of the Old Plantation*, 1905
- *A Treasury of Jewish Folklore: Stories, Traditions, Legends, Humor, Wisdom and Folk Songs of the Jewish People*, 1948
- *Up Cutshin and Down Greasy: Folkways of a Kentucky Mountain Family*, 1959
- *We Always Lie to Strangers: Tall Tales from the Ozarks*, 1951

400
Languages

Why Weed Languages?

The language section in school library media collections is often static in spite of the dynamic need for global communications today. Which of these antonyms best describes your language collection: static or dynamic? In other words, was it "groovy" decades ago but not "fantasmic" now?

Dewey Numbers to Check

You will need to check all your 400s (Language), including the reference section. Most of your titles will probably be in the 420s (English), but check the remainder of the 400 section for other languages (430s for German, 440s for French, etc.). Your AV and professional collections should also be checked.

Specific Criteria for Weeding

Within each specific language you will first come across the etymologies (4_2s) with titles on the origin and development of words in that language. Older titles are still fine if they are in good shape and have an attractive presentation that will appeal to the casual reader as well as those working on reports. Dictionaries (4_3s) need to be current, especially in the home language. Do a couple of test searches on current words (hazmat, metadata, Wi-Fi, etc.) to make sure they are up to date. Titles in the 4_7s (word variations: historical, geographical, and modern) are where the books on slang are located. These are high-interest titles if kept current.

The 4_8s (usage and linguistics) will have more titles in foreign languages compared to English (428s). Keep the more popular foreign languages (French, Spanish, German) current with attractive and easy-to-use language guides that will support the foreign-language programs in your area.

Tips for Replacing Titles

In addition to the languages traditionally taught in schools, consider introducing a few titles on some other languages (Chinese, Arabic, etc.) that are becoming so important vocationally in today's world.

Consider Weeding Titles Like These

- [ ] *30 Days to a More Powerful Vocabulary*, 1970
- [ ] *101 Words and How They Began*, 1979
- [ ] *American Talk: Where Our Words Came From*, 1977
- [ ] *Appleton's New Cuyas English-Spanish and Spanish-English Dictionary*, 1966
- [ ] *Babar's French Lessons = Les Leçons de Français de Babar*, 1963
- [ ] *Beyond the Dictionary in Spanish: A Handbook of Colloquial Usage*, 1964
- [ ] *Brave New Words: The Newest, Funniest, and Most Original Dictionary in the World*, 1979
- [ ] *A Browser's Dictionary, and Native's Guide to the Unknown American Language*, 1980
- [ ] *Collins Contemporary Spanish Dictionary: Spanish-English, Inglés-Español*, 1970
- [ ] *A Concise Dictionary of English Idioms*, 1975
- [ ] *The Concise Oxford Dictionary of Current English*, 1964
- [ ] *Crowell's Dictionary of English Grammar and Handbook of American Usage*, 1928
- [ ] *Dictionary of Afro-American Slang*, 1970
- [ ] *A Dictionary of American Idioms*, 1975
- [ ] *Dictionary of American Slang*, 1960
- [ ] *Dictionary of Americanism: A Glossary of Words and Phrases Usually Regarded as Peculiar to the United States*, 1968
- [ ] *How to Learn Languages and What Languages to Learn*, 1973
- [ ] *Idiom's Delight: Curious Imagery in Everyday Language—Spanish, French, Italian, Latin*, 1988
- [ ] *Language in America*, 1970
- [ ] *Language in the Modern World*, 1960
- [ ] *Language Today: A Survey of Current Linguistic Thought*, 1967
- [ ] *Linguistics Today*, 1969
- [ ] *Modern American Grammar and Usage*, 1956
- [ ] *Opportunities in Foreign Language Careers*, 1975
- [ ] *The Traveler's Dictionary: A Compact Dictionary of Commonly Used Words and Phrases in French, German, Italian, and Spanish*, 1985

507.8
Science Experiments

Why Weed Science Experiments?

There is at least one "given" in the life of a school library media center: Teachers will assign science fair projects and students will come looking for ideas and assistance. Some students will be eager and others will face the assignment with dread. Serve them all with current materials. Be sure that no student takes home a book and hears her or his parent say, "I remember using this same book when I was in school!"

Dewey Numbers to Check

Most titles on science fair projects will be in 507.8 (Use of Apparatus and Equipment in Study and Teaching). But you may have titles on science experiments that will be found across the 500s and 600s. You will also need to check the reference and AV collections.

Specific Criteria for Weeding

First, look at the publication dates on titles dealing with science experiments and science fair projects. Although some experiments are classic across the years, the methods and safety standards may have changed. In addition to safety concerns, older titles may have dated illustrations that work against the content. And the illustrations in those older titles often show bias as to gender and race.

Next look at the subject areas suggested for the experiments. Many students will need help in deciding on their subject. Current areas of interest should be represented. For example, yesterday's student may have been satisfied with weather topics such as cold fronts while today's student is more intrigued by the effects of El Niño, La Niña, hurricanes, and global warming.

Tips for Replacing Titles

Look for new titles with current suggestions on successfully demonstrating a science experiment or competing with a science fair project. Although an overhead projector or a poster display might have worked ten or twenty years ago, today's student might be more successful (and comfortable!) with a website or a multimedia presentation.

Consider Weeding Titles Like These

- *200 Science Experiments for Boys and Girls*, 1974
- *Air Pollution Experiments for Junior and Senior High School Science Classes*, 1968
- *Anti-pollution Lab: Elementary Research, Experiments and Science Projects on Air, Water and Solid Pollution in Your Community*, 1975
- *Developing a Science Fair Project* [filmstrip], 1972
- *Electricity Experiments for Children*, 1968
- *Experiments in Visual Science for Home and School*, 1966
- *Exploring Science in Your Home Laboratory*, 1963
- *Fun with Science: Easy Experiments for Young People*, 1956
- *The Golden Book of Chemistry Experiments: How to Set Up a Home Laboratory—Over 200 Simple Experiments*, 1960
- *How to Be a Scientist at Home*, 1972
- *How to Do a Science Project*, 1974
- *It's Fun to Know Why: Experiments with Things around Us*, 1952
- *Materials and Elements: Science Projects and Experiments for the Junior Scientist*, 1964

- *Mr. Wizard's Experiments for Young Scientists*, 1959
- *New Ideas for Science Fair Projects*, 1967
- *Practical Classroom Science Experiments: A Collection of 150 Science Experiments*, 1967
- *Research Ideas for Young Scientists*, 1958
- *Science Experiments for the Space Age*, 1972
- *Science Projects Handbook*, 1960
- *Scientific Research Projects for High School Students*, 1975
- *See for Yourself: A First Book of Science Experiments*, 1952
- *Tomorrow's World of Science: The Challenge of Today's Experiments*, 1964
- *The True Book of Science Experiments*, 1961
- *What Happens If . . . ? Science Experiments You Can Do by Yourself*, 1974
- *Your Science Fair Project*, 1965

510
Mathematics

GENERAL WEEDING GUIDELINES

500s
5 to 15 years

700s
5 to 10 years

Why Weed Mathematics?

When did you last purchase a really good book or AV title on mathematics? When did you last read a report on American students lagging in math skills? School library media collections certainly are not to blame, but maybe an aggressive weeding and replacement plan in mathematics would help spark some student interest and achievement.

Dewey Numbers to Check

Most of the titles on general mathematics will be found in the 510s (Mathematics). Titles on specific branches of math will be found in the 512s–519s (Algebra–Probabilities). Titles on math puzzles will be found at 793.74 (Mathematical Games and Recreations). Professional titles on mathematics education are in the 372.7s (Elementary Education, Mathematics). There will also be some titles scattered in the 640s (Home and Family Management) and the 650s (Management) that deal with consumer and business math. Check the reference and AV collections also.

Specific Criteria for Weeding

In an area such as mathematics that is not subject to dramatic changes in content over the years, it is easy to allow the collection to stagnate. Although content is still a consideration (but make sure you don't still have titles on "new math"), you will be looking more at presentation, physical condition, and format as criteria in weeding the mathematics titles.

Presentation and physical condition are very important here. Old and boring appearance translates to "old and boring subject" to students. Old AV formats (such as filmstrips) may serve only to accommodate old lesson plans and do not generate any student enthusiasm or learning.

Tips for Replacing Titles

Look for new print titles using new publishing trends (sidebars, etc.) to attract student interest. Consider purchasing some how-to titles on the popular new Sudoku number puzzles, available now even at the elementary level. Replace old filmstrips with new AV formats.

Consider Weeding Titles Like These

- *400 Group Games and Activities for Teaching Math*, 1978
- *Achieve with Mathematics*, 1978
- *Addition and Subtraction Are Brothers* [sound recording], 1973
- *Adventures in Mathematics*, 1967
- *Algebra: A Modern Introduction*, 1965
- *Applied Business Mathematics for Consumer and Business Use*, 1965
- *Applied Mathematics for Girls*, 1963
- *Arithmetic for Successful Living*, 1955
- *Background Math for a Computer World*, 1980
- *Basic Math Skills for Everyday Life* [filmstrip], 1977
- *Basic Mathematics for Technical Occupations*, 1976
- *Breakthroughs in Mathematics*, 1963
- *Bulletin Board Displays for Mathematics*, 1967
- *Bulletin Boards for the New Math*, 1965

- *The Case of the Missing Chickcows: Adding Positive and Negative Integers* [filmstrip], 1975
- *The Changing Curriculum: Mathematics*, 1967
- *College Entrance Review in Mathematics Aptitude*, 1961
- *Comprehensive Math Review for the High School Equivalency Examination*, 1975
- *Computer Math Experience: Programs and Exercises for Use in the Computer-Equipped Classroom*, 1970
- *Consumer and Career Mathematics*, 1978
- *Consumer Math* [filmstrip], 1976
- *Funny Number Tricks: Easy Magic with Arithmetic*, 1976
- *The I Hate Mathematics! Book*, 1975
- *Mathematics at the Farm*, 1978
- *Mathematics in the Kitchen*, 1978

520
Space and Astronomy

GENERAL WEEDING GUIDELINES

500s
5 to 15 years

Biography
5 to 10 years

Fiction
5 to 15 years

Why Weed Space and Astronomy?

Students today grew up having seen images of men walking on the moon (the first walk was in 1969). If interested in the space program, they might know that NASA is now planning to return to the moon—projected to be in 2018. So, how does your collection support students' interest in space as the last frontier? Make sure you don't have embarrassing titles such as *Tomorrow the Moon* (published in 1959) or other offenders.

Dewey Numbers to Check

Check the 520s (Astronomy and Allied Sciences) in both the circulating and the reference sections. Next check the biography section for famous names in space explanations and explorations. Review the AV collection and try to locate fiction titles with a central topic of space exploration.

Specific Criteria for Weeding

From the launch of the first successful weather satellite in 1960 to NASA's ambitious plans announced in 2005 to return to the moon in 2018, the field of space and astronomy moves very quickly and with a lot of national and international news attention. Any titles on space exploration that were published closer to that 1960 date should not be in your collection. Many space topics also have a natural conclusion that should be reflected in titles on those subjects: the Mir space station launched by the Soviets in 1986 was "de-orbited" in 2001, the Hubble space telescope story is incomplete without references to its defects, the *Columbia* shuttle program that began in 1981 ended in tragedy with its twenty-eighth mission in 2003. Make sure the titles you keep in your collection tell the complete story. Also, provide an international balance by including materials on the Russian contribution and the recent entry of China (in partnership with India) into space exploration. All titles on our solar system may be outdated soon if the recent discovery of the tenth planet is confirmed. Regardless of the status of this new "planet" that is bigger than Pluto (the last planet identified, in 1930), titles on the solar system should include some of the recent debate on what qualifies as a planet.

Tips for Replacing Titles

In addition to adding current titles to support what is new in space exploration, try to add interesting biographies on the famous space names such as John Glenn, Neil Armstrong, Sally Ride, and Eileen Collins.

Consider Weeding Titles Like These

- ☐ *50 Facts about Space*, 1983
- ☐ *2000 Years of Space Travel*, 1963
- ☐ *Astronomy from Space: Sputnik to Space Telescope*, 1983
- ☐ *Astronomy in the Space Age* [filmstrip], 1968
- ☐ *Atlas of the Moon: Astronomy, Astronautics*, 1964
- ☐ *A Book of Moon Rockets for You*, 1964
- ☐ *Dictionary of Astronomy, Space, and Atmospheric Phenomena*, 1982
- ☐ *Earth and the Universe* [filmstrip], 1976
- ☐ *Earth, Moon, Sun, and Space* [filmstrip], 1985
- ☐ *Exploring Space: How Astronomers Study the Universe* [videorecording], 1978
- ☐ *Going to the Moon* [kit], 1978
- ☐ *The Golden Book of Astronomy: A Child's Introduction to the Wonders of Space*, 1959
- ☐ *Intelligent Life in Space*, 1962
- ☐ *Introducing Astronomy* [filmstrip], 1983

- ☐ *Moon Flights*, 1985
- ☐ *My First Book about Space: A Question and Answer Book*, 1982
- ☐ *The New Astronomy: Probing the Secrets of Space*, 1982
- ☐ *The New Space Encyclopaedia: A Guide to Astronomy and Space Exploration*, 1973
- ☐ *Race for the Moon*, 1979
- ☐ *Secrets of the Universe* [filmstrip], 1976
- ☐ *Space: A Fact and Riddle Book*, 1978
- ☐ *The Space Encyclopaedia: A Guide to Astronomy and Space Research*, 1958
- ☐ *Space Science: A New Look at the Universe*, 1967
- ☐ *Watchers of the Skies: An Informal History of Astronomy from Babylon to the Space Age*, 1966
- ☐ *You and Space Neighbors*, 1953

551.2
Earthquakes and Volcanoes

Why Weed Earthquakes and Volcanoes?

Earthquakes and volcanoes have been in the news recently because of the devastating tsunami that resulted from the Indonesia earthquake in December 2004, and the 2005 quake in Pakistan. Statistically, the number of earthquakes and volcanoes has not increased over the years, but media coverage and public attention have increased. Take advantage of this new interest and refresh your collection in this area.

**GENERAL WEEDING
GUIDELINES**

500s
5 to 15 years

Dewey Numbers to Check

Titles on earthquakes, volcanoes, and tsunami activity are shelved near each other: 551.21 (Volcanoes), 551.22 (Earthquakes), and 551.46 (Hydrosphere and Submarine Geology) for waves and tsunamis (moved from the earlier classification of 551.47). Review the reference and AV collections also.

Specific Criteria for Weeding

Worldwide major earthquakes and volcanoes that have been in the news should be included in titles on this topic in your collection. Check the timeline (if available) in a book to see the year it stops. Nationally, Mt. St. Helens in the state of Washington continues to be of interest and in the news since its eruption in 1980. Alaska and California contain some of the most seismically active regions in the world, so be sure your titles are up to date in this high-interest area. (Florida, Iowa, North Dakota, and Wisconsin are the least seismically active states in the United States!) Replace older books and AV titles with attractive and interesting new ones that have updated timelines, events, and predictions.

Tips for Replacing Titles

Because the scientific knowledge behind these geological events continues to improve, look for new titles that provide up-to-date information in addition to descriptions of events and their resulting damage. Also, information on improved methods to predict and provide warnings for earthquakes and volcanoes as well as tsunamis will be of interest to readers.

Consider Weeding Titles Like These

- *About Earthquakes*, 1957
- *All About Volcanoes and Earthquakes*, 1953
- *Causes of Catastrophe: Earthquakes, Volcanoes, Tidal Waves and Hurricanes*, 1948
- *Chains of Fire: The Story of Volcanoes*, 1966
- *A Child's Book of Mountains and Volcanoes*, 1954
- *The Circle of Fire: The Great Chain of Volcanoes and Earth Faults*, 1968
- *Earthquakes: A Natural History*, 1974
- *Earthquakes: A Primer*, 1978
- *Earthquakes and Moving Continents* [filmstrip], 1978
- *Earthquakes: New Scientific Ideas about How and Why the Earth Shakes*, 1972
- *The First Book of Volcanoes and Earthquakes*, 1972
- *The Making of the Earth: Volcanoes and Continental Drift*, 1974
- *Mountains of Fire: An Introduction to the Science of Volcanoes*, 1962
- *Mt. St. Helens: A Volcano Erupts* [filmstrip], 1980
- *Natural Disasters and What to Do* [filmstrip], 1976
- *Our Dynamic Planet* [filmstrip], 1978
- *Science Book of Volcanoes*, 1969
- *Volcanoes in Action: Science and Legend*, 1962
- *Volcanoes in History, in Theory, in Eruption*, 1962
- *Volcanoes: New and Old*, 1946
- *We Are the Earthquake Generation: Where and When the Catastrophes Will Strike*, 1979
- *Why the Earth Quakes*, 1969
- *Will California Fall into the Sea?* 1972
- *Wonders of Nature* [filmstrip], 1970

551.6
Weather

Why Weed Weather?

Everybody talks about the weather, watches it on TV, and reads about it. Worldwide there is a common interest in the weather because it impacts everyone's daily life. The interest in weather has not changed over the years, but the science of weather forecasting has. Current technology has drastically altered how weather is forecasted and how storms are tracked. Your collection on weather will be used for general interest as well as curriculum support.

Dewey Numbers to Check

Weather is an easy topic to review for weeding. Look in the 551.6s (Climatology and Weather) to evaluate your titles. Check the reference and AV collections also.

Specific Criteria for Weeding

When you evaluate your collection on weather, you will be checking to see if you have current weather technology represented as well as accurate accounts of past weather events and disasters. The science of weather forecasting should include today's radar and weather satellite technology. Some weather conditions (such as El Niño) that are in the news today are not in older weather books. Environmental concerns involving the ozone layer, the greenhouse effect, and pollution are now recognized as having an impact on our weather, both daily and long term.

Carefully review any titles on meteorology as a career to make sure they are not out of date and misleading to students. Also look at the illustrations or visuals in any print or AV item for dated equipment (such as typewriters instead of computers) and people unless they are intended to represent a specific period in history.

Tips for Replacing Titles

Think back to the last major weather-related event that affected your community or received extensive national coverage. Hurricane? Tornado? Flood? Be sure you purchase titles covering that event when available.

Consider Weeding Titles Like These

- About Our Weather, 1964
- The Air Around Us: Man Looks at His Atmosphere, 1967
- Ask Me a Question about the Weather, 1966
- The Atmosphere in Action, 1965
- Climate, 1969
- Climate and Weather, 1969
- Disastrous Hurricanes and Tornadoes, 1981
- The First Book of Weather, 1956
- Forecasting the Weather [filmstrip], 1979
- Historical Catastrophes: Hurricanes and Tornadoes, 1972
- Hurricanes: Monster Storms from the Sea, 1973
- Hurricanes, Storms, Tornadoes, 1968
- Hurricanes: Weather at Its Worst, 1967
- The Killer Storms, 1970
- Meteorology: An Introduction, 1981
- Storm Alert: Understanding Weather Disasters, 1980
- Storms and Man, 1971
- Storms from Inside Out, 1973
- Weather: A Guide to Phenomena and Forecasts, 1965
- Weather All Around Us, 1966
- Weather Instruments: How They Work, 1968
- Weather on the Move, 1970
- What Does a Meteorologist Do? 1981
- What Makes the Wind, 1982
- What's Happening to Our Climate? 1978

567.9
Dinosaurs

Why Weed Dinosaurs?

While trying to keep up with the rapidly changing modern world, it is easy to neglect to weed areas long regarded as fixed in time. However, current research often changes long-held beliefs. Dinosaurs are a good example of this. Scientists know a great deal more about dinosaurs than they did even five or ten years ago. Weeding this section might make a great research project for older students if you can enlist their help.

Dewey Numbers to Check

General titles on dinosaurs will be in the 567.9s (Reptiles), while individual types of dinosaurs will be in the 567.91s (Specific Dinosaurs and Other Archosaurs). Remembering that young people learn many facts from fiction, check your fiction titles where dinosaurs are central to the theme. Also check the reference and AV collections.

Specific Criteria for Weeding

Any titles that show people and dinosaurs living at the same time give the wrong impression to young students! Over 60 million years passed between the age of dinosaurs and the first signs of humans on earth. Dinosaurs did not eat grass—it hadn't evolved yet! Not all dinosaurs lived at the same time either. Although there are dozens of theories on why dinosaurs became extinct, there is now widespread evidence that a meteorite impact was at least the partial cause.

Check the illustrations of dinosaurs. Are the tails of all the dinosaurs depicted as low and dragging behind them? Scientists now believe that a more accurate posture would be with the tails held high. Much of what we thought we knew about dinosaurs was speculation. There continues to be much debate and new discoveries about dinosaurs and their age.

Tips for Replacing Titles

Since young children especially love materials on dinosaurs, many titles are automatically weeded due to wear and hard use. Older titles that are still in good condition probably aren't appealing to your students. Consider discarding and replacing them with some of the new attractive titles continually published.

Consider Weeding Titles Like These

- [ ] *After the Dinosaurs*, 1968
- [ ] *All About Strange Beasts of the Past*, 1956
- [ ] *Amazing World of Dinosaurs* [filmstrip], 1977
- [ ] *Animals of Long Ago*, 1976
- [ ] *Animals: Prehistoric and Present* [filmstrip], 1978
- [ ] *Archosauria: A New Look at the Old Dinosaur*, 1979
- [ ] *Baby Brontosaurus*, 1988
- [ ] *Before and After Dinosaurs*, 1959
- [ ] *The Big, Big Egg*, 1963
- [ ] *Book to Begin on Dinosaurs*, 1959
- [ ] *Bruno Brontosaurus*, 1983
- [ ] *Como y Porque de los Dinosaurios*, 1972
- [ ] *The Day of the Dinosaur*, 1968
- [ ] *Dinosaur Book: The Ruling Reptiles and Their Relatives*, 1951
- [ ] *Dinosaurs and Other Prehistoric Animals*, 1972
- [ ] *The Evolution and Ecology of the Dinosaurs*, 1975
- [ ] *The How and Why Wonder Book of Dinosaurs*, 1960
- [ ] *How Can We Find Out about Dinosaurs?* 1973
- [ ] *Know Your Dinosaurs*, 1977
- [ ] *A Natural History of Dinosaurs*, 1977
- [ ] *Now You Know about Dinosaurs*, 1977
- [ ] *Reptiles: Past and Present*, 1976
- [ ] *The True Book of Dinosaurs*, 1955
- [ ] *What Really Happened to the Dinosaurs?* 1967
- [ ] *The Wonders of the Dinosaur World*, 1936

576
Genetic Engineering

**GENERAL WEEDING
GUIDELINES**

100s
5 to 10 years

500s
5 to 15 years

600s
5 to 15 years

Why Weed Genetic Engineering?

Genetic engineering is of high interest today, and it is one of the fastest-developing sciences. Case in point: The U.S. Human Genome Project began in 1990 with a projected completion date of 2005 (fifteen years). But because of the rapidly developing technology in the field, the project was completed early—in 2003. Can you justify keeping materials in your collection that are twenty years old or more?

Dewey Numbers to Check

Older titles in genetics will be found at 576 (Genetics and Evolution) but newer titles on genetic engineering will be in the 660.6s (Biotechnology). Check both areas. Agricultural genetics is found at 631.5 (Cultivation and Harvesting). Titles on the ethics of genetic engineering are found in the 174s (Occupational Ethics). Check the reference and AV collections also.

Specific Criteria for Weeding

Genetic engineering is a relatively new science, emerging only since the discovery of DNA in the 1950s. The good news here is that you won't have books on this topic published before 1950 hiding on your shelves! But new sciences tend to develop faster than older ones. With this in mind, you should critically review all titles more than five years old.

The relationship of ethics to genetic engineering has been an issue from the beginning. Cloning, test-tube babies, and stem cell research have always raised ethical concerns. Older titles that are missing current developments in the news will not give students a true picture.

Another continuing topic of interest is the impact of genetics on diseases. Aside from school research, there will always be some students interested for purely personal reasons, such as a family member with a genetically related disease.

Tips for Replacing Titles

A new issue of interest is the genetic engineering of our food supply. Be sure your collection includes titles on this topic.

Consider Weeding Titles Like These

- [ ] *Bio-Revolution: DNA and the Ethics of Man-Made Life*, 1978
- [ ] *The Cloning of Man: A Brave New Hope—or Horror?* 1978
- [ ] *The Ethics of Genetic Control: Ending Reproductive Roulette*, 1974
- [ ] *Fabricated Man: The Ethics of Genetic Control*, 1970
- [ ] *From Cell to Clone: The Story of Genetic Engineering*, 1979
- [ ] *Genetic Controversy* [filmstrip], 1981
- [ ] *Genetic Engineering: Man and Nature in Transition*, 1974
- [ ] *Genetic Engineering: Prospects for the Future* [videorecording], 1985
- [ ] *Genetic Engineering: The Nature of Change* [videorecording], 1984
- [ ] *Genetic Engineering: Threat or Promise?* 1976
- [ ] *Genetic Politics: The Limits of Biological Control*, 1979
- [ ] *Genetic Revolution: Shaping Life for Tomorrow*, 1974
- [ ] *Genetics* [filmstrip], 1983
- [ ] *The Genetics Explosion*, 1980

- [ ] *Genetics in Medicine*, 1966
- [ ] *Genetics of Livestock Improvement*, 1963
- [ ] *Human Engineering: Marvel or Menace?* 1978
- [ ] *Improving on Nature: The Brave New World of Genetic Engineering*, 1977
- [ ] *Life from the Lab: Progress and Peril* [video-recording], 1981
- [ ] *Man-Made Life: An Overview of the Science, Technology, and Commerce of Genetic Engineering*, 1982
- [ ] *Recombinant DNA: The Untold Story*, 1978
- [ ] *Reshaping Life: Key Issues in Genetic Engineering*, 1985
- [ ] *Splicing Life: A Report on the Social and Ethical Issues of Genetic Engineering with Human Beings*, 1982
- [ ] *Tool for Tomorrow: New Knowledge about Genes*, 1979
- [ ] *Who Should Play God? The Artificial Creation of Life and What It Means for the Future of the Human Race*, 1977

576.8
Evolution

**GENERAL WEEDING
GUIDELINES**

200s
10 to 15 years

500s
5 to 15 years

Biography
5 to 10 years

Why Weed Evolution?

Today, many state departments of education have removed the word *evolution* from their state curriculum standards and replaced it with more vague terminology, such as *change over time*. As sensitive as this topic is in many localities, be sure the titles in your collection are current, critically approved, educationally sound, and defendable should a challenge arise.

Dewey Numbers to Check

Look at the 576.8s (Evolution) and then move to the biography section for the bulk of titles on evolution and its important personalities. Continue reviewing the 171s (Ethical Systems), and for titles on evolution versus creation, look at the 202s (Doctrines) as well as the 291.2s (currently unassigned) for older titles on this controversy. The reference, AV, and professional collections should also be reviewed.

Specific Criteria for Weeding

The post-*Sputnik* renewal of emphasis on science in the schools, combined with generous federal library media funding, resulted in many titles on evolution being added to school library media centers in the 1960s and 1970s. Court cases (such as *Epperson v. Arkansas* in 1968) further supported the teaching of evolution. Publishers responded to the demand. Then, opponents of the evolution theory (creationists, young earth creationists, and intelligent design proponents) wrote books for this K–12 market as well. In addition, more titles were marketed that approached the topic by "teaching the controversy."

Your collection might have some or all of these points of view. Critically look at all of them to see if they are still in print (a good sign), give information in the best possible presentation, and are not relics of some past personal persuasion or gift to the collection.

Tips for Replacing Titles

All grade levels will have some titles on Charles Darwin. Consider updating yours with newer and more appealing biographies and reviews of his work. Upper-level grades should also have an attractive new edition of Darwin's original work, a very readable scientific work for students.

Consider Weeding Titles Like These

- [ ] *Adam's Ancestors: The Evolution of Man and His Culture*, 1960
- [ ] *After Man: A Zoology of the Future*, 1981
- [ ] *Animal Species and Their Evolution*, 1963
- [ ] *Apes, Angels, and Victorians: The Story of Darwin, Huxley, and Evolution*, 1963
- [ ] *Beginning of the Beginning: An Unfolding Story of How Nature and Life Evolved on Our Planet*, 1971
- [ ] *The Big Bang: The Creation and Evolution of the Universe*, 1980
- [ ] *Charles Darwin: Pioneer in the Theory of Evolution*, 1964
- [ ] *Controversy in the Twenties: Fundamentalism, Modernism, and Evolution*, 1969
- [ ] *Creation and Evolution: Myth or Reality?* 1982
- [ ] *The Creation-Evolution Controversy (Implications, Methodology and Survey of Evidence): Towards a Rational Solution*, 1984
- [ ] *Did the Devil Make Darwin Do It? Modern Perspectives on the Creation/Evolution Controversy*, 1983
- [ ] *Evolution and Genetics: The Modern Theory of Evolution*, 1962
- [ ] *Heredity, Evolution, and Society*, 1976
- [ ] *Monkeys, Apes, and Man* [videorecording], 1971
- [ ] *The New Evolutionary Timetable: Fossils, Genes, and the Origin of Species*, 1981
- [ ] *Race, Evolution, and Mankind*, 1966
- [ ] *The Right Size: Why Some Creatures Survive and Others Are Extinct*, 1968
- [ ] *Scientists Confront Creationism*, 1983
- [ ] *The Story of Life: From the Big Bang to You*, 1980
- [ ] *Three Billion Years of Life: The Drama of Evolution* [videorecording], 1976
- [ ] *Understanding Evolution*, 1966
- [ ] *The Way to Modern Man: An Introduction to Human Evolution*, 1968
- [ ] *Where Do You Come From? The Story of Evolution*, 1967
- [ ] *Why Things Change: The Story of Evolution*, 1973
- [ ] *You and How the World Began*, 1960

577
Ecology

**GENERAL WEEDING
GUIDELINES**

300s
5 to 20 years

500s
5 to 15 years

Why Weed Ecology?

Everyone recognizes ecology as one of the critical issues in today's world, and yet sound ecological practices are not a part of most of our everyday living habits. Students in elementary through high school are more receptive than any other age group to the ecology message. School library media collections should support that enthusiasm with current titles on ecology.

Dewey Numbers to Check

Most of the titles on ecology will be found in the 570s, newer titles at 577 (Ecology), and older titles at the now unassigned 574. There will also be some titles scattered in the 304.2s (Human Ecology), the 333s (Economics of Land and Energy), and the 372.35s (Science and Technology/Elementary Education). Review the reference and the AV collections also.

Specific Criteria for Weeding

A lot of books published in the 1970s and 1980s on this topic are still on the shelves of school library media centers. Even if their content is still somewhat accurate, the style and presentation are surely dated. Students noticing that a book published twenty or thirty years ago contains dire warnings may end up thinking it more of a Chicken Little message instead of a legitimate concern today. Replace these old titles with current recommended publications that are up to date in content and contemporary in presentation.

AV collections must be carefully reviewed also as to format as well as content and presentation. Discard (in an ecologically responsible manner, of course) any outdated AV formats such as filmstrips.

Tips for Replacing Titles

Look for replacement titles on this topic that contain new ecological issues (such as global warming) that are not addressed in many of the older publications.

Consider Weeding Titles Like These

- [ ] *Americans and Environment: The Controversy over Ecology*, 1971
- [ ] *The Arthur Godfrey Environmental Reader*, 1970
- [ ] *Career Opportunities: Ecology, Conservation, and Environmental Control*, 1971
- [ ] *Change in Alaska: People, Petroleum, and Politics*, 1971
- [ ] *Changing Scene: An Ecology Story*, 1975
- [ ] *Cities Fit to Live In and How We Can Make It Happen: Recent Articles on the Urban Environment*, 1971
- [ ] *City and Suburb: Exploring an Ecosystem*, 1975
- [ ] *Compact City: A Plan for a Livable Urban Environment*, 1973
- [ ] *Conservation through Recycling: From Pollutant to Product* [filmstrip], 1971
- [ ] *Dash McTrash and the Pollution Solution: Learning to Care about Ecology* [filmstrip], 1972
- [ ] *Eco-catastrophes—The Risk We Take with Our Environment* [filmstrip], 1975
- [ ] *The Ecology Controversy: Opposing Viewpoints*, 1973
- [ ] *Ecology: Man's Effects on His Environment and Its Mechanisms*, 1971
- [ ] *Ecology: Modern Biology Series*, 1963
- [ ] *Ecology: Understanding the Crisis* [filmstrip], 1972
- [ ] *Energy: Here Today, Gone Tomorrow* [filmstrip], 1974
- [ ] *The Environment of America: Present/Future/Past*, 1971
- [ ] *Guide to Films (16 mm) about Ecology, Adaptation and Pollution*, 1971
- [ ] *The Land We Live On: Restoring Our Most Valuable Resource*, 1971
- [ ] *The Last Days of Mankind: Ecological Survival or Extinction*, 1971
- [ ] *Living in Cities: Psychology and the Urban Environment*, 1975
- [ ] *Living Things in the City* [filmstrip], 1968
- [ ] *Man and the Changing Earth* [filmstrip], 1973
- [ ] *Our Polluted World: The Price of Progress* [filmstrip], 1972
- [ ] *Planet in Peril: Man and the Biosphere Today*, 1972

597
Reptiles and Amphibians

Why Weed Reptiles and Amphibians?

Many times school library media centers concentrate on giving students what they need and not what they want (our apologies to the Rolling Stones!), so sometimes it's fun to turn that around. And throughout the years, students have been interested in reptiles. Make sure your titles in this area have not stayed the same—weed and refresh! Give them what they want!

Dewey Numbers to Check

This is a quick and easy topic to check—just go to 597 (Cold-Blooded Vertebrates) and you will find amphibians at 597.8 and reptiles at 597.9. You may also have some titles on reptiles as pets in the 639.3s (Culture of Cold-Blooded Vertebrates). Also check the reference and AV collections.

Specific Criteria for Weeding

Reptiles and amphibians are not rapidly changing subject areas, so reviewing content for accuracy is not as much of an issue with these older titles. However, any information that addresses endangered species status must be checked for current accuracy.

The main criteria for weeding here are the condition of the titles and the presentation of the material. Old titles that are much loved and used by students have to be in bad condition from all that use! Weed and replace them with new attractive titles. If some of your older titles are still in very good condition, they are probably lacking in visual appeal and should be weeded also.

The AV collection is another story. Older titles survive here because of the more limited and controlled circulation. In fact, you may have some videos that were converted from old 16 mm movies, making them even older than the packaging date indicates. Review the presentation here, both for dated visual images and play quality.

Tips for Replacing Titles

There are lots of new titles available that are fun to look at in addition to being educational. Select some with great illustrations and watch them fly off the shelves.

Consider Weeding Titles Like These

- [ ] *The Age of Reptiles: Life in Prehistoric Times*, 1958
- [ ] *All About Snakes*, 1956
- [ ] *All Color Book of Reptiles*, 1974
- [ ] *Creepy, Crawly Things: Reptiles and Amphibians*, 1977
- [ ] *Endangered Species: Reptiles and Amphibians* [picture], 1976
- [ ] *Fascinating Snakes of North America* [filmstrip], 1970
- [ ] *Field Book of Snakes of North America and Canada*, 1941
- [ ] *A Field Guide to Reptiles and Amphibians of Eastern and Central North America*, 1958
- [ ] *A First Look at Snakes, Lizards, and Other Reptiles*, 1975
- [ ] *Getting to Know Reptiles and Amphibians* [filmstrip], 1979
- [ ] *The How and Why Wonder Book of Reptiles and Amphibians*, 1973
- [ ] *I Can Read about Reptiles*, 1973
- [ ] *The Illustrated Book about Reptiles and Amphibians of the World*, 1960

- [ ] *Keeping Amphibians and Reptiles as Pets*, 1972
- [ ] *Living Reptiles of the World*, 1957
- [ ] *Looking at Reptiles* [videorecording], 1964
- [ ] *The Natural History of North American Amphibians and Reptiles*, 1955
- [ ] *The New Field Book of Reptiles and Amphibians*, 1970
- [ ] *Poisonous Snakes of the World: A Manual for Use by U.S. Amphibious Forces*, 1970
- [ ] *The Reptile World: A Natural History of the Snakes, Lizards, Turtles, and Crocodilians*, 1978
- [ ] *Reptiles and Amphibians* [filmstrip], 1978
- [ ] *Reptiles and Amphibians: Based on the Television Series, Wild, Wild World of Animals*, 1976
- [ ] *Reptiles and Their World*, 1961
- [ ] *Reptiles around the World*, 1957
- [ ] *Reptiles: Past and Present*, 1976

600
Vocational Trades

GENERAL WEEDING GUIDELINES

300s
5 to 20 years

600s
5 to 15 years

Why Weed Vocational Trades?

Library media collections in K–12 schools can be very important to non–college-bound students when making vocational decisions. Accurate and current information on vocational trades (both career and how-to books) is critical to young people making life work decisions. Job outlooks, work environments, and training in all the trades have changed dramatically over the years. Make sure your collection is up to date.

Dewey Numbers to Check

Vocational trade materials will be found throughout the 600s (Technology, Applied Science)—from allied medical occupations in the 610s (Medicine and Health) to carpentry in the 698s (Detail Finishing). Occupational training and vocational schools will be found at 370.113 (Vocational Education). Vocational guidance materials are located at 371.4 (Student Guidance and Counseling). There will also be some vocational titles scattered across the collection with the subject areas and in the fiction section. The AV collection should be reviewed as well as any separate career collections.

Specific Criteria for Weeding

Currency, accuracy, bias, and physical appearance are all weeding criteria for this topic. And currency is the prime consideration. Misleading a student into a dead-end career is a serious mistake! You can't predict the future, but you should have the most current information available. For example, do you have titles on travel agents and retail shopping that do not consider the impact of the Internet on these careers? Look for dated photographs as well as dated information when reviewing titles.

Accuracy is difficult to judge across a wide range of occupations, but it is very important. If you are not sure of projections for work conditions, wages, and the like in certain vocations, find someone who can help you make those evaluations. Bias is another consideration. Do you have titles on car repair that show only men in the illustrations? Do the titles on nursing show only women at work?

Tips for Replacing Titles

Build a collection that exposes students to a wide range of ever-changing career choices and opportunities.

Consider Weeding Titles Like These

- [ ] *Agricultural, Forestry, and Oceanographic Technicians,* 1969
- [ ] *Aim for a Job as an Electronic Technician,* 1978
- [ ] *Aim for a Job in Automotive Service,* 1968
- [ ] *Aim for a Job in the Iron and Steel Industry,* 1967
- [ ] *Architectural and Building Trades Dictionary,* 1950
- [ ] *The Art and Science of Manicuring,* 1960
- [ ] *Automotive Service Business: Operations and Management,* 1973
- [ ] *Basic Fingerwaving* [motion picture], 1969
- [ ] *Behind the Scenes at an Oil Field,* 1959
- [ ] *Blueprint Reading for the Building Trades,* 1955
- [ ] *Bright Future Careers with Computers,* 1969
- [ ] *Careers in a Fire Department,* 1977
- [ ] *Careers in Trucking,* 1979
- [ ] *Clinical Nurse Specialist,* 1970
- [ ] *Construction: Industry and Careers,* 1976

- [ ] *Dictionary of Technical Terms, Containing Definitions of Commonly Used Expressions in Aeronautics, Architecture, Woodworking and the Building Trades, Electrical and Metalworking Trades, Printing, Chemistry, Plastics, Etc.,* 1964
- [ ] *Dressmaking Techniques for Trade Students,* 1970
- [ ] *Estimating for the Building Trades,* 1965
- [ ] *Exploring Careers in Hospitality and Food Service,* 1975
- [ ] *Fashion Buying and Merchandising,* 1976
- [ ] *History and Trends of Practical Nursing,* 1966
- [ ] *Park Ranger: Equipment, Training, and Work of the National Park Ranger,* 1971
- [ ] *Psychiatric Nursing,* 1968
- [ ] *Your Future in Automotive Service,* 1968

613.2
Nutrition

Why Weed Nutrition?

Nutrition is closely linked to learning ability as well as to overall health. Poor nutrition leads to poor school performance. Your collection on nutrition might have stayed the same over the past years, but current surveys show that the nutrition habits of today's students have become worse. It's time to evaluate the old titles and replace them with new materials to reach students "where they live."

Dewey Numbers to Check

Titles on nutrition will be found at 613.2 (Dietetics) and with cookbooks at 641 (Food and Drink). Review the reference and AV collections also.

Specific Criteria for Weeding

Look first at the publication dates on titles dealing with nutrition. If they were published in the 1960s or 1970s, they are from a different world. Yes, we had fast-food restaurants then, but not on every corner. Yes, we had TV, but not hundreds of channels on cable and certainly not the Internet! One thing we did have more of in those days was physical activity—both at school and at home. Nutrition information for today should address this new sedentary lifestyle.

Even some of the basic nutrition facts have changed over the years, resulting in today's recommendations for less meat and fats but more fruits and vegetables in our diets. Examine the content of your titles on nutrition to make sure the information is timely. That old food pyramid has completely changed!

Also look at the content to see if current dietary issues are addressed. Although it is true that more and more students (even elementary age) are overweight, it is also true that various eating disorders unheard of twenty years ago impact a large number of our students—including many at your school.

Tips for Replacing Titles

Students need to be aware of the dangers of today's fad diets and of eating disorders. There is no shortage of popular new titles on dieting being released today. Try to provide some balance and sound information.

Consider Weeding Titles Like These

- [ ] *The ABCs of Vitamins, Minerals, and Natural Foods*, 1972
- [ ] *Clean Plates: Cooking for Young Children*, 1964
- [ ] *The Complete Book of Food and Nutrition*, 1961
- [ ] *Controlling Your Weight*, 1973
- [ ] *Eat Well on a Dollar a Day: Live a Healthier Life at a Fraction of the Cost*, 1975
- [ ] *Everyone's Guide to Better Food and Nutrition*, 1974
- [ ] *Everywoman's Diet Handbook*, 1975
- [ ] *Fad Diets Can Be Deadly: The Safe, Sure Way to Weight Loss and Good Nutrition*, 1975
- [ ] *The Family Guide to Better Food and Better Health*, 1971
- [ ] *Food and Nutrition* [filmstrip], 1975
- [ ] *Food Facts and Fallacies: The Intelligent Person's Guide to Nutrition and Health*, 1965
- [ ] *Food Facts for Young People*, 1968
- [ ] *Food for Modern Living*, 1967
- [ ] *Food for Teens: Snacks That Count* [filmstrip], 1972
- [ ] *Guide to Modern Meals*, 1964
- [ ] *How to Be a Wise Shopper: More Meat for Your Money* [filmstrip], 1973
- [ ] *How to Get the Most for Your Food Dollar*, 1970
- [ ] *Let's Talk about Food: Answers to Your Questions about Foods and Nutrition*, 1974
- [ ] *Meals for the Modern Family*, 1961
- [ ] *Mowry's Basic Nutrition and Diet Therapy*, 1975
- [ ] *The No Fad Good Food $5 a Week Cookbook*, 1974
- [ ] *Nutrition and Physical Fitness*, 1973
- [ ] *Nutrition for Today*, 1973
- [ ] *Teenage Diet, Nutrition, and Exercise* [filmstrip], 1974
- [ ] *The Teenager's Guide to Diet and Health*, 1964

613.7
Physical Fitness

Why Weed Physical Fitness?

The month of May is National Physical Fitness and Sports Month, but every month of the year has news releases about the declining physical fitness of Americans—including those of K–12 school age. We are all constantly urged to get in shape! How about working on your physical fitness titles to get that collection in shape?

Dewey Numbers to Check

Most titles on this topic will be at 613.7 (Physical Fitness). Take a minute to check 796.41 (Weight Lifting) to be sure the titles there are focused on athletics instead of fitness. Bodybuilding for fitness should be at 613.7, while bodybuilding for contests or athletics should be at 796.41. And while you are at it, make sure there are no old titles on this topic still at 646.7 where bodybuilding was once classed. If you find some that are worth keeping, move them to 613.7 or 796.41, depending on the focus. Check your reference and AV collections also.

Specific Criteria for Weeding

As important as the topic of physical fitness is in schools today, the circulation of print titles will be driven mainly by the appeal of the works and not by required reports. Look at the illustrations to see if they are relevant to your students. If they are not, there's no reason to keep the book regardless of the content. Check all titles to see if they are up to date, with current nutritional, diet, and exercise recommendations. Students (and staff) are hearing these messages in the news almost daily; they will want only recent information.

Gender bias should be considered also. For example, working with weights is not just for boys anymore. It's considered important for girls as well. Finally, review all your "celebrity" titles. A personality that you associate with fitness may have a completely different connotation (or none at all) for your students.

Tips for Replacing Titles

Your problem in adding new titles on this topic will be choosing from the tremendous number on the market currently. Talk to your students (and staff) to see what they are interested in now. Check the reviews, order, and then promote your new "in shape" fitness collection.

Consider Weeding Titles Like These

- *Anyone for Fitness?* [videorecording], 1978
- *Better Physical Fitness for Girls*, 1964
- *Bodyworks: The Kids' Guide to Food and Physical Fitness*, 1981
- *The Boy's Book of Physical Fitness*, 1973
- *Bruce Jenner's The Athletic Body: A Complete Fitness Guide for Teenagers— Sports, Strength, Health, Agility*, 1984
- *The Complete Manual of Fitness and Well-Being*, 1988
- *Christie Brinkley's Outdoor Beauty and Fitness Book*, 1983
- *The Complete Encyclopedia of Weight Loss, Body Shaping, and Slenderizing*, 1980
- *Denise Austin's 1-Minute Exercises: The Only Personal Trainer You'll Ever Need*, 1987
- *Discovering Lifetime Fitness: Concepts of Exercise and Weight Control*, 1984
- *Doctor Soloman's Proven Master Plan for Total Body Fitness and Maintenance*, 1976
- *The Every Other Day Exercise Book: The Easy-Does-It Program for Better Bodies*, 1977
- *Everybody's a Winner: A Kid's Guide to New Sports and Fitness*, 1976

- *Exercise: What It Is, What It Does*, 1982
- *Fit for Life: Suzy Prudden's Complete Program for Getting and Staying Fit for Life*, 1978
- *Fun to Be Fit* [filmstrip], 1984
- *Heavyhands: The Ultimate Exercise System*, 1982
- *Jane Fonda's Prime Time Workout* [videorecording], 1984
- *Modern Bodybuilding: A Complete Guide to the Promotion of Fitness, Strength and Physique*, 1970
- *The New Aerobics: The World's Most Popular Physical Fitness Program*, 1970
- *The New Art of Keeping Fit: Modern Methods for Men*, 1963
- *Olympic Athletes Ask Questions about Exercise and Nutrition*, 1977
- *Shape Up: The New Unisex Bodybuilding*, 1978
- *Slim Goodbody* [filmstrip], 1978
- *Toughen Up! A Boy's Guide to Better Physical Fitness*, 1963

613.85
Tobacco Education

GENERAL WEEDING GUIDELINES

300s
5 to 20 years

600s
5 to 15 years

Why Weed Tobacco Education?

Preteens and teenagers make their decisions on tobacco use based on peer pressure, persuasive tobacco images and packaging, and antismoking campaigns. Peer pressure and social images stay current. Unfortunately, much of the antismoking information readily available in school library media centers is too dated to be credible to young people. Check your collection for outdated tobacco education titles, and "weed 'em if you've got 'em!"

Dewey Numbers to Check

Look in the 613.85s (Tobacco) for titles on the health values of avoiding tobacco products. Titles on the physiological effects of tobacco and cessation methods are found in the 616.86s (Substance Abuse under Diseases of the Nervous System and Mental Disorders). Tobacco as a social issue because of its addictive nature is found in the 362.29s (Substance Abuse under Mental and Emotional Illnesses and Disturbances). Check your reference and AV collections also.

Specific Criteria for Weeding

Presentation is critical in tobacco education materials. Any message the student reads, hears, or sees in this area is reinforced (or countered) by his or her world. Although the antismoking message has stayed relatively consistent for the last twenty years, the world has not. Print or AV titles with outdated illustrations (clothing, hair, family structure, cars) should be discarded even if the text is still fairly accurate.

Content is the second weeding criterion. Even if it seems accurate, does it reflect today's knowledge? Is there up-to-date information on the connection of tobacco use to diseases? On the effects of secondhand smoke on allergies, pregnancy, and low-birth-weight babies? On smokeless tobacco products? Also, make sure practical and current advice for quitting smoking is included.

Tips for Replacing Titles

Weed any filmstrip on this topic (if it's a filmstrip, it's too old), then carefully examine all other AV titles on tobacco education. Make it a priority to replace them with current AV titles with solid messages and attractive presentations that will make an impression on your students.

Consider Weeding Titles Like These

- [ ] *Alcohol, Tobacco, and Drugs: Their Use and Abuse*, 1977
- [ ] *Cigarette Country: Tobacco in American History and Politics*, 1971
- [ ] *Clearing the Air: Perspectives on Environmental Tobacco Smoke*, 1988
- [ ] *A Doctor's Book on Smoking and How to Quit*, 1977
- [ ] *Don't Let Smoking Kill You!* 1957
- [ ] *Dying to Smoke*, 1964
- [ ] *Everything You Wanted to Know about Smoking, but Were Afraid to Ask*, 1980
- [ ] *Helping Youth Avoid Four Great Dangers: Smoking, Drinking, VD, and Narcotics Addiction*, 1965
- [ ] *It's Really Up to You: You and Smoking*, 1970
- [ ] *The Joy of Quitting: How to Help Young People Stop Smoking*, 1979
- [ ] *Let's Learn About Tobacco* [filmstrip], 1983
- [ ] *Nicotine: An Old Fashioned Addiction*, 1985
- [ ] *Smoke Screen: Tobacco and the Public Welfare*, 1963
- [ ] *Smoking: A Research Update* [videorecording], 1984

- [ ] *Smoking and Your Life*, 1964
- [ ] *Smoking, Health, and Personality*, 1965
- [ ] *Smoking: Your Choice between Life and Death*, 1970
- [ ] *Smokeless Tobacco: It Can Snuff You Out* [videorecording], 1986
- [ ] *Tobacco and Alcohol: The $50,000 Habit* [kit], 1967
- [ ] *Tobacco and Americans*, 1960
- [ ] *Tobacco and Your Health: The Smoking Controversy*, 1969
- [ ] *Up in Smoke: How Smoking Affects Your Health* [videorecording], 1982
- [ ] *When and How to Quit Smoking*, 1964
- [ ] *Women and Smoking*, 1972
- [ ] *Young People and Smoking: The Use and Abuse of Cigarette Tobacco*, 1964

614.5
AIDS

GENERAL WEEDING GUIDELINES

300s
5 to 20 years

600s
5 to 15 years

Why Weed AIDS?

Do you still have titles on AIDS (Acquired Immune Deficiency Syndrome) that were published in the 1980s? That was the decade that brought us the name of the disease for the first time (1981), personalized it with famous names (Rock Hudson, 1985), and shocked us with the loss of a friend or neighbor. Twenty years ago we bought books and AV materials on this topic and many of those titles may still be on the shelves of library media centers. They contain outdated information and may lead students to think of the disease as part of their parents' generation, not theirs.

Dewey Numbers to Check

Check the 614.5s (Incidence of and Public Measures to Prevent Specific Diseases and Kinds of Diseases) for materials on prevention as well as the spread and control of AIDS. Check the 616.97s (Diseases of Immune System) for specific information on this disease. For titles on living with AIDS and services available to patients, look at the 362.196s (Services to Patients with Specific Diseases). Check the reference and AV collections as well as your biography section.

Specific Criteria for Weeding

Currency of information is critical in any discussion of treatment and drug regimens for HIV/AIDS. Any materials older than the advances of the early 2000s should not be kept, and even those should convey the message that treatment is still a rapidly changing and developing field.

Information about preventing infection has not changed as much as medical treatments have over the years, but the faces of those most likely to be infected have changed: from middle-class white males in the 1980s to today's women, minority groups, and senior citizens. Check the style of the prevention information to see that it is not dated and that any illustrations are not misleading.

Tips for Replacing Titles

Students paying attention to current news and celebrity benefits may think that AIDS is just a problem in another part of the world. But the number of new cases nationally proves that wrong. Be sure you obtain a balanced collection that shows the threat both nationally and globally.

Consider Weeding Titles Like These

- [ ] *AIDS and the Law: A Guide for the Public,* 1987
- [ ] *AIDS and the Third World,* 1989
- [ ] *AIDS: Distinguishing between Fact and Opinion,* 1989
- [ ] *AIDS: Everything You Must Know about Acquired Immune Deficiency Syndrome, the Killer Epidemic of the '80's,* 1983
- [ ] *The AIDS File: What We Need to Know about AIDS Now!* 1987
- [ ] *AIDS Questions and Answers for Kids,* 1987
- [ ] *AIDS: Trading Fears for Facts: A Guide for Teens,* 1989
- [ ] *Coping with AIDS: Facts and Fears,* 1988
- [ ] *Don't Get It: Teenagers and AIDS* [videorecording], 1988
- [ ] *The Essential AIDS Fact Book: Expanded and Updated with New Information on Treatment,* 1989
- [ ] *Everything You Need to Know about AIDS,* 1988
- [ ] *Gay: What Teenagers Should Know about Homosexuality and the AIDS Crisis,* 1987
- [ ] *Lynda Madaras Talks to Teens about AIDS: An Essential Guide for Parents, Teachers, and Young People,* 1988
- [ ] *Mobilizing Against AIDS: The Unfinished Story of a Virus,* 1986

- [ ] *The Plague Years: A Chronicle of AIDS, the Epidemic of Our Times,* 1986
- [ ] *Preventing AIDS: A Practical Guide for Everyone,* 1987
- [ ] *Protection against Infection: The Inside Story of the Immune System and AIDS* [videorecording], 1988
- [ ] *Questions and Answers on AIDS,* 1987
- [ ] *The Truth about AIDS: Evolution of an Epidemic,* 1985
- [ ] *Understanding AIDS: A Comprehensive Guide,* 1985
- [ ] *Understanding AIDS: What Teens Need to Know* [videorecording], 1988
- [ ] *What to Do about AIDS: Physicians and Mental Health Professionals Discuss the Issues,* 1986
- [ ] *When Someone You Know Has AIDS: A Practical Guide,* 1987
- [ ] *You Can Do Something about AIDS,* 1988
- [ ] *Young People and AIDS* [videorecording], 1989

616
Diseases

**GENERAL WEEDING
GUIDELINES**

300s
5 to 20 years

600s
5 to 15 years

Why Weed Diseases?

Students turn to library media materials on diseases for more than completing school assignments and reports. Home and personal circumstances often prompt a student to seek information on various diseases. However, improvements in technology and treatments have drastically changed prognoses and the way people cope with diseases. In the treatment of most diseases, amazing progress has been made in the past five years. Any title older than ten years is certainly suspect and should be reviewed carefully.

Dewey Numbers to Check

Most of the titles on the clinical nature of diseases will be found in the 616s (Diseases). Check the 362.1s (Physical Illness) for titles focusing more on the medical care and treatment for people with diseases. Check your AV and reference collections also. Remembering that students learn from fiction, check your fiction titles where characters' illnesses are central to the theme and the time frame could be mistaken for modern.

Specific Criteria for Weeding

The most obvious example for weeding in this area is the topic of sexually transmitted diseases. If you have materials on this topic printed prior to the 1980s, AIDS is not included. Even titles published in the late 1980s will have outdated and misleading information on this disease.

Titles with information on diabetes should be reviewed carefully because dietary guidelines have been modified in recent years. Cancer treatment and research now include gene therapy and tests that were not available just a few years ago. Additional hepatitis viruses have been identified in recent years. That development, along with treatment changes, makes older titles candidates for weeding.

Tips for Replacing Titles

Look for news reports of current disease outbreaks and treatments and try to follow them with well-reviewed titles. An example is tuberculosis. Just a few years back, tuberculosis was thought of as a conquered disease, but we are seeing outbreaks recently even in our school-age population.

Consider Weeding Titles Like These

☐ *Borrowing Time: Growing Up with Juvenile Diabetes*, 1979

☐ *Cancer: A New Breakthrough*, 1972

☐ *Cancer: The Silent Stigma* [filmstrip], 1978

☐ *Choices: Realistic Alternatives in Cancer Treatment*, 1980

☐ *Communicable and Infectious Diseases: Diagnosis, Prevention, Treatment*, 1964

☐ *The Conquest of Tuberculosis*, 1964

☐ *Coronary: Prediction and Prevention*, 1978

☐ *Critical Areas of Health* [filmstrip], 1966

☐ *Current Respiratory Care*, 1977

☐ *Diabetes: A Practical New Guide to Healthy Living*, 1981

☐ *The Diabetic at Work and Play: A Modern Manual for Diabetics with the Latest Information on Oral Drugs, Diabetic Camps, Research, and Many Other Topics*, 1971

☐ *Facts about VD for Today's Youth*, 1973

☐ *For People Who Make Love: A Doctor's Guide to Sexual Health*, 1975

☐ *"Herpie": The New VD Around Town* [filmstrip], 1977

☐ *How to Avoid Social Diseases: A Practical Handbook*, 1973

☐ *The Invisible Chain: Diseases Passed On by Inheritance*, 1972

☐ *Male Trouble: A New Focus on the Prostate*, 1976

☐ *Modern Woman's Medical Encyclopedia*, 1966

☐ *New Hope for Incurable Diseases*, 1971

☐ *The New Way to Live with Diabetes*, 1966

☐ *The Teenager and VD: A Social Symptom of Our Times*, 1969

☐ *Tuberculosis: A Half-Century of Study and Conquest*, 1970

☐ *VD: The Twentieth Century Plague* [filmstrip], 1975

**GENERAL WEEDING
GUIDELINES**

600s
5 to 15 years

629.1
Aviation History

Why Weed Aviation History?

Sometimes you weed a section of your collection to refresh as much as up-date. The 2003 centennial celebration of the Wright brothers' famous first flight in 1903 resulted in a publishing frenzy of titles on early aviation as well as the Wrights. Now that the frenzy is over, it's a good time to review what you have on this topic and select the best of the recently published titles.

Dewey Numbers to Check

Look in the 629.1s (Aerospace Engineering) for most titles on the general subject of early aviation and the history of its development. Much of this history of early aviation is focused on those early pioneers in the field, especially the Wright brothers and Amelia Earhart—check your biography section for works on them. Look in both the individual and the collective biographies. Also check the reference and the AV collections.

Specific Criteria for Weeding

When looking at general history titles on aviation, be especially aware of the title compared to the publication date. You may find some "complete histories" that were published about the same time that you or your students' parents were born!

Check the physical condition of older biographies of Wilbur and Orville Wright because they have probably had years of heavy use for reports. There are so many new and attractive titles now to replace those old worn ones. However, keep a copy of Fred C. Kelly's biography, *The Wright Brothers*, because it is the only biography authorized (and reviewed) by Orville Wright. But replace older worn editions with new editions still in print.

Tips for Replacing Titles

Amelia Earhart biographies should be updated because of the continuing controversy over her disappearance. Was it a war conspiracy? Aliens? An escape to New Jersey? Make sure your titles give the full story and watch for new developments in this continuing saga.

Consider Weeding Titles Like These

- *1001 Questions Answered about Aviation History*, 1969
- *Air Facts and Feats*, 1978
- *All About Aviation*, 1964
- *Amelia Earhart: Pioneer of Aviation*, 1973
- *Aviation and Space Dictionary*, 1974
- *Aviation Careers*, 1977
- *Aviation Electronics*, 1970
- *Aviation in the Modern World: The Dramatic Impact upon Our Lives of Aircraft, Missiles, and Space Vehicles*, 1960
- *Aviation: The Complete Book of Aircraft and Flight*, 1980
- *Aviation: The Complete Story of Man's Conquest of the Air*, 1978
- *Ceiling Unlimited: The Story of American Aviation from Kitty Hawk to Supersonics*, 1953
- *The Complete Illustrated Encyclopedia of the World's Aircraft*, 1978
- *Contributions of Women: Aviation*, 1975
- *Flight through the Ages*, 1974
- *Flying Army: The Modern Air Arm of the U.S. Army*, 1971

- *Flying: An Introduction to Flight, Airplanes, and Aviation Careers*, 1980
- *From Flying Horse to Man on the Moon: A History of Flight from Its Earliest Beginning to the Conquest of Space*, 1963
- *A History of the World's Airlines*, 1964
- *The How and Why Wonder Book of Airplanes and the Story of Flight*, 1974
- *Reaching into Space: The Story of Flight* [filmstrip], 1980
- *The Sky's the Limit: Women Pioneers in Aviation*, 1979
- *Take Me Out to the Airfield! How the Wright Brothers Invented the Airplane*, 1976
- *Wings in Your Future: Aviation for Young People*, 1960
- *Wings: The Complete Encyclopedia of Aviation*, 1977
- *The Wright Brothers: Pioneers of American Aviation*, 1950

**GENERAL WEEDING
GUIDELINES**

600s
5 to 15 years

641.5
Cooking

Why Weed Cooking?

Cookery is a subject area that often does not receive much attention in weeding activities. Cookbooks are often kept on the shelves until their physical condition qualifies them for removal. In the meantime, there have been substantial changes in the recommended procedures for safely cooking and storing food. Dietary guidelines have also seen dramatic changes in the past few years. Students interested in cooking—and good nutrition—deserve information that reflects these changes.

Dewey Numbers to Check

Check the entire 641 (Food and Drink) section, but especially the general cookbooks found at 641.5 (Cooking). Vegetarian cookbooks are found at 641.6 (Cooking Specific Materials) and baking and barbecuing books at 641.7 (Specific Cooking Processes and Techniques). Other specialty cookbooks such as appetizers, salads, and sandwiches are at 641.8 (Cooking Specific Kinds of Dishes). Check the reference and the AV collections also.

Specific Criteria for Weeding

Millions of cases of foodborne illnesses are reported each year. Bacteria in food (especially from undercooked meat, poultry, and fish) can cause intestinal distress, hospitalization, and even death. *Salmonella, Campylobacter*, and *E. coli* are among the bacteria that have redefined the way foods must be safely prepared. Older methods of cooking (such as rare hamburgers) can result in serious health problems for the user. Even when safety in food handling and preparation is not at issue, new dietary guidelines make many cookbooks obsolete and even dangerous to young cooks. Carefully review cookbooks with recipes that disregard fat intake, sugar, salt, and cholesterol. Special-diet cookbooks should also be carefully reviewed to make sure they have not been outdated by current dietary information.

Tips for Replacing Titles

Update some of the old classic cookbooks with newer editions when available. Add some vegetarian cookbooks that are attractive and contain practical and tasty recipes. Eating more vegetarian meals would be good for everyone, but teenagers are often the ones most willing to give vegetarian dishes a try. Replace older vegetarian cookbooks with attractive new ones to encourage this interest.

Consider Weeding Titles Like These

- *365 Ways to Cook Hamburger*, 1960
- *The Allergy Cookbook: Delicious Recipes for Every Day and Special Occasions*, 1969
- *The Art of Cooking for the Diabetic*, 1977
- *Better Homes and Gardens Home Canning Cook Book*, 1973
- *The Betty Betz Teen-Age Cookbook*, 1953
- *Betty Crocker's New Boys and Girls Cookbook*, 1965
- *Bland but Grand: A Cookbook for People on Certain Continuing Diets*, 1969
- *Caring and Cooking for the Allergic Child*, 1974
- *A Cookbook for Girls and Boys*, 1946
- *Cool, Chill, and Freeze: A New Approach to Cookery*, 1973
- *Delicious Seafood Recipes*, 1953
- *The Delicious World of Raw Foods: A Culinary Guide to Preparing Appetizers, Soups, Salads, Vegetables, Main Dishes, and Desserts with Little or No Cooking*, 1977
- *Diabetic Menus, Meals and Recipes*, 1977
- *Enjoying Food on a Diabetic Diet*, 1974
- *Food for Modern Living*, 1967
- *Good Food for Bad Stomachs: 500 Delicious and Nutritious Recipes for Sufferers from Ulcers and Other Digestive Disturbances*, 1951
- *Guide to Modern Meals*, 1964
- *Home Canning, the Last Word: Newer and Better Methods for Top Quality*, 1976
- *Home Preserving Made Easy: A Complete Guide to Pickling, Smoking, Canning, Drying, Freezing, and Jelly-Making*, 1975
- *Joy of Cooking*, 1964
- *Meals for the Modern Family*, 1961
- *Modern Encyclopedia of Cooking: A Modern Cook Book, Complete in Every Detail, Brings the Latest Developments in Home Economics into Your Kitchen for a Simpler, Better, and Richer Life*, 1955
- *Pressure Cooker Cookbook*, 1978
- *Roundup of Beef Cookery: A Complete Guide to the Best Beef Recipes from the Ranch Kitchens of America*, 1960
- *Stay Slim for Life: Diet Cookbook for Overweight Millions*, 1958

740
Hobbies and Crafts

GENERAL WEEDING GUIDELINES

700s
5 to 10 years

Why Weed Hobbies and Crafts?

Some hobbies such as stamp and coin collecting have been around forever and have changed very little. Likewise, crafts such as needlework, pottery, basket making, and origami still require the same basic skills. However, the passage of time continues to bring new styles to old ways. These new styles and presentations are often critical in attracting young readers.

Dewey Numbers to Check

Most of the hobbies and crafts books will be found in the 745s (Decorative Arts) and 746s (Textile Arts). However, you will have to survey all the 700s to pick up activities such as stamp collecting (769.56), sport card collecting (796s), and photography (770s). Check the reference and AV collections also.

Specific Criteria for Weeding

Because many hobby and craft how-to books can continue to have useful information and appeal to readers over the years, weed and replace any books that are in poor physical condition. Then look at the publication dates on books that are guides to collectibles. A book published ten years ago will be missing ten years of those stamps, coins, and the like to collect! Beanie Babies were hot a few years ago, but there might be little interest now. Sport card collectors are looking for new heroes like A-Rod and Dante Culpepper—or even newer ones. Listen to what your students tell you about their hobbies and crafts.

Continue weeding by looking at the books that are in good physical condition but are not circulating. These older titles may be so dated in appearance (including the clothing and hairstyles in illustrations) that they have little appeal to students. Older books may also be giving bad information if they include pricing for supplies or purchasing.

Tips for Replacing Titles

Consider adding holiday craft titles that include a broader range of holiday traditions such as Hanukkah and Kwanzaa. Look for illustrations in all books that include both boys and girls instead of supporting a traditional gender bias.

Consider Weeding Titles Like These

- [ ] *50 Gifts to Make for Under $1.00*, 1974
- [ ] *African Crafts for You to Make*, 1969
- [ ] *Better Homes and Gardens Treasures from Throwaways*, 1976
- [ ] *Camping and Camp Crafts*, 1964
- [ ] *Click: A First Camera Book*, 1979
- [ ] *Coin Collecting for Fun and Profit*, 1964
- [ ] *Contemporary Ceramics* [filmstrip], 1983
- [ ] *Corrugated Carton Crafting*, 1972
- [ ] *Creating from Scrap*, 1962
- [ ] *Designer Crafts*, 1978
- [ ] *Electronic Games*, 1982
- [ ] *Fun with Next to Nothing*, 1963
- [ ] *Hobbies*, 1972
- [ ] *How to Have Fun with Needlepoint*, 1974
- [ ] *Joy of Crafts*, 1975
- [ ] *Lettering Art in Modern Use*, 1965
- [ ] *Low Fire: Other Ways to Work in Clay*, 1980

- [ ] *Macrame, Knitting and Weaving*, 1974
- [ ] *Making Pictures without Paint*, 1973
- [ ] *Sew It! Wear It!* 1975
- [ ] *A Simplified Guide to Collecting American Coins*, 1959
- [ ] *Stamp Collectors Guide*, 1965
- [ ] *Taking Pictures*, 1977
- [ ] *The Teenagers Guide to Collecting Practically Anything*, 1972
- [ ] *The Women's Day Book of Weekend Crafts*, 1978

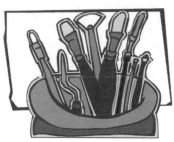

741
Drawing and Cartooning

Why Weed Drawing and Cartooning?

Drawing and cartooning have been popular with students over the years. Techniques may not have changed much over those years, but the style of drawing and cartooning has changed along with students. The strong interest in graphic novels today is a good example of that change of style.

Dewey Numbers to Check

Check the 741s (Drawing and Drawings) to find most titles on drawing and cartooning. You may have some titles at 742 (Perspective in Drawing). Although the reference collection might not have any titles on this topic, the AV collection probably does have some that should be reviewed.

Specific Criteria for Weeding

The instructions for drawing various animate and inanimate objects may not have changed much over the years, but those objects might have! Look at your how-to-draw books from the students' point of view. That horse may still look like a horse, but does that car, truck, or spacecraft look familiar to today's students?

Look also at the background around the actual drawing or cartooning instructions. Do the illustrations include out-of-date fashions and appearances on models or the instructor? Kids will notice this. Gender is another issue to consider. If the illustrations seem to steer boys to certain subjects and girls to others, replace or update with newer titles or editions.

Tips for Replacing Titles

Comic books and instructive books on drawing have new appearances and names now. Young students are probably more interested in Spider-Man types than Superman. Adding popular graphic novels and new art forms such as Japanese manga will help bring your collection up to date for older students.

Consider Weeding Titles Like These

- ☐ *Aim for a Job in Cartooning*, 1976
- ☐ *Basic Drawing* [filmstrip], 1979
- ☐ *Cartooning Fundamentals*, 1957
- ☐ *Cartooning the Head and Figure*, 1967
- ☐ *The Complete Book of Cartooning*, 1977
- ☐ *Draw 50 Airplanes, Aircrafts and Spacecraft*, 1977
- ☐ *Draw 50 Famous Faces*, 1978
- ☐ *Drawing and Selling Cartoons*, 1964
- ☐ *Drawing Cars*, 1964
- ☐ *Drawing for Boys*, 1956
- ☐ *Drawing for Girls*, 1960
- ☐ *Drawing People in Action*, 1961
- ☐ *Editorial and Political Cartooning: From Earliest Times to the Present*, 1976
- ☐ *How to Do Cartooning and Animation* [filmstrip], 1975
- ☐ *How to Draw Cartoons Successfully: 46 Practical Lessons*, 1935
- ☐ *How to Draw Comics the Marvel Way*, 1978
- ☐ *How to Draw Costumes and Clothes*, 1964
- ☐ *How to Draw Military and Civilian Uniforms*, 1965
- ☐ *How to Draw People at Work*, 1970
- ☐ *How to Draw Spaceships*, 1979
- ☐ *Make Your Own Comics for Fun and Profit*, 1975
- ☐ *New Things to Draw and How to Draw Them*, 1959
- ☐ *Objective Drawing Techniques: New Approaches to Perspective and Intuitive Space*, 1966
- ☐ *Shorthand Fashion Sketching*, 1956
- ☐ *Sketching with the Felt-Tip Pen: A New Artist's Tool*, 1959

770
Photography

Why Weed Photography?

Remember that camera you were using for family photos ten years ago? Compare that to the digital camera you are using today. Big change, right? If your library media collection titles on photography have not changed in the last ten or twenty years, the students are not getting what they need to maintain an interest and answer their questions in this subject area.

Dewey Numbers to Check

Review general photography titles at 770 (Photography, Photographs, Computer Art). Also check the remaining 770s, from 771 (Techniques, Procedures, Apparatus, Equipment, Materials) for works on specific camera types to 779 (Photographs). The biography section should be checked for those titles not classed in the 770s. Review the reference and AV collections also.

Specific Criteria for Weeding

Because of the rapid changes in consumer-level cameras in recent years, review carefully any title over ten years old. Most students today are using and are more interested in digital cameras and digital video techniques than 35 mm or videotape-based models or others such as instant Polaroids, early underwater cameras, or pinhole cameras. You will want to keep historical accounts of older cameras and their inventors (George Eastman and Edwin Land, for example), but you do not need titles that are selection guides to outdated cameras and equipment. Darkroom methods and techniques probably also belong in photography history books instead of guides, although photography requiring a darkroom may be a hobby for some of your students and their parents. Keep newer books on the basics for them, but make sure the section on safely storing and using chemicals is accurate. Careers in photography and titles about photography as a business must be current to be relevant today.

Tips for Replacing Titles

Technical advances date most photography books quickly, but classic photographs keep their appeal. Consider adding some titles on the works of famous photographers such as Ansel Adams, Margaret Bourke-White, Robert Capa, Henri Cartier-Bresson, Anne Geddes, Annie Leibovitz, Alfred Stieglitz, and William Wegman.

Consider Weeding Titles Like These

- [ ] *101 Experiments in Photography*, 1969
- [ ] *Advanced Black and White Printing* [video-recording], 1978
- [ ] *All About 35mm Photography: A Complete Guide to Choosing and Using 35mm Cameras and Equipment*, 1979
- [ ] *All-in-One Movie Book: The Complete Guide to Super 8*, 1972
- [ ] *Basic Photography: A Step-by-Step Introduction to Camera Equipment, Exposures, Composition, Developing, Printing, Finishing, Flash Techniques*, 1977
- [ ] *Beginner's Guide to Darkroom Techniques*, 1976
- [ ] *Beginning Underwater Photography*, 1975
- [ ] *The Complete Beginner's Guide to Photography*, 1979
- [ ] *The Darkroom Handbook: A Complete Guide to the Best Design, Construction, and Equipment*, 1979
- [ ] *Electronic Flash Photography: A Complete Guide to the Best Equipment and Creative Techniques*, 1980
- [ ] *Freelance Photography: Advice from the Pros*, 1979
- [ ] *The History of Photography: From 1839 to the Present Day*, 1971
- [ ] *How to Make Good Pictures: An Entertaining Authoritative Handbook for Everyone Who Takes Pictures*, 1972

- [ ] *How to Take Better Polaroid Pictures*, 1975
- [ ] *Modern Photographic Techniques*, 1976
- [ ] *Money-Making Photography*, 1980
- [ ] *Photo Fun: An Idea Book for Shutterbugs*, 1973
- [ ] *Photo Reports Make It Happen* [video-recording], 1978
- [ ] *Photographic Tricks Simplified: A Modern Photo Guide*, 1974
- [ ] *Photography: How to Develop Film* [slide], 1978
- [ ] *Planning and Producing Slide Programs*, 1978
- [ ] *The Student Journalist and Creative Photography*, 1976
- [ ] *Traveling with Your Camera: Creative 35 mm Photography*, 1965
- [ ] *Trick Photography: Crazy Things You Can Do with Cameras*, 1980
- [ ] *Your Future in Photography*, 1970

780
Music

**GENERAL WEEDING
GUIDELINES**

700s
5 to 10 years

Biography
5 to 10 years

Why Weed Music?

Music speaks to all students, though not all types of music create the same amount of interest or effect. A strong music collection will attract students to music they already enjoy and introduce them to music yet to be appreciated. A music collection with outdated popular music will not appeal to students. Even worse, a collection with old and physically unattractive titles can reinforce any negative mental images of classical or older music.

Dewey Numbers to Check

Most of the music books will be found in the 780s (Music). Biographical titles of musicians and composers should be checked in both the individual and collective sections. Also check the reference and AV sections.

Specific Criteria for Weeding

The first things to look at in your music collection are the titles themselves. A title that leads a student to believe that the item is about current popular music but is several years (or decades) old will only invite contempt. Weed misleading titles and do not purchase works with titles that will date themselves before their time! Next look at the publication dates. Even if the subject area is almost timeless, the approach to the subject may be dated, inaccurate, or just plain offensive. Career material, ethnic collections, and gender emphasis are prime examples.

The wonderful ethnic heritage of music must be preserved in a sensitive manner. Look especially at gender- or ethnicity-specific illustrations and content that might be offensive now. Finally, look at the physical condition and the circulation history of each title. Very popular titles showing heavy physical wear should be updated or replaced in order to maintain their appeal to students. Titles not circulating may be unattractive in format, illustrations, or reading level.

Tips for Replacing Titles

Many students dream of a life in the music world. Advice on forming bands and developing careers must be current to today's music scene. Look for current titles that will help budding musicians set good career goals.

Consider Weeding Titles Like These

- [ ] *The Agony of Modern Music, 1955*
- [ ] *American Composers Today: A Biographical and Critical Guide, 1940*
- [ ] *American Pop, 1969*
- [ ] *America's Music: From the Pilgrims to the Present, 1955*
- [ ] *Black Music in America, 1971*
- [ ] *Careers and Opportunities in Music, 1964*
- [ ] *Composers of Today: A Comprehensive Biographical and Critical Guide to Modern Composers of All Nations, 1934*
- [ ] *Contemporary Composers, 1918*
- [ ] *Encyclopedia of Folk, Country, and Western Music, 1983*
- [ ] *Exploring Careers in Music, 1982*
- [ ] *Famous Modern Conductors, 1954*
- [ ] *Famous Negro Music Makers, 1955*
- [ ] *Golden Guitars: The Story of Country Music, 1972*
- [ ] *Great Modern Composers, 1941*
- [ ] *How Music Grew: From Prehistoric Times to the Present Day, 1939*
- [ ] *How to Form a Rock Group, 1968*
- [ ] *Inside Pop: America's Top Ten Groups, 1968*
- [ ] *The Language of the Music Business: A Handbook of Its Customs, Practices and Procedures, 1965*
- [ ] *Men of Popular Music, 1944*
- [ ] *Modern Composers for Boys and Girls, 1941*
- [ ] *Music Education for Teenagers, 1966*
- [ ] *Music Makers of Today, 1958*
- [ ] *The New Encyclopedia of Music and Musicians, 1937*
- [ ] *The Story behind Popular Songs, 1958*
- [ ] *This Modern Music: A Guide for the Bewildered Listener, 1957*

792.8
Dance

**GENERAL WEEDING
GUIDELINES**

700s
5 to 10 years

Biography
5 to 10 years

Why Weed Dance?

Most of your students like dance or dance music—especially in the styles that suit the interests of their peer groups. But do they have a broader appreciation for dance that will prompt them to continue this activity as they grow older? Maybe they get that exposure at home and maybe not. Try to keep your dance titles broad and current to encourage a lifelong interest.

Dewey Numbers to Check

This is an easy area to check. Review the 792.8s (Ballet and Modern Dance) and the 793.3s (Social, Folk, National Dancing). Check any biographies classed here as well and those in the individual and collective biography sections. Review the reference and AV collections also.

Specific Criteria for Weeding

Dance is a very personal thing for many students—they love their dance styles and dismiss the rest as old, boring, uninteresting, or worse! Look at your dance titles to see if they invite contempt from students. Currency is critical here for popular forms. Beyond popular, other forms of dance should be presented in an interesting format or they will just reinforce the notion that they are not worth investigating.

Too many times the passion for dancing passes along with youth. Students need to know a variety of styles of dance that they can respect and continue to enjoy through adulthood. Examine your dance titles to see if they prompt giggles on your part—then think of how your students would react.

Tips for Replacing Titles

Look for new titles that include the current DanceSport interest and projected Olympic recognition. Update dance titles as a social recreation for those students enjoying dance reality TV shows and competitions.

Consider Weeding Titles Like These

- [ ] *116 Modern Dance Classroom Combinations*, 1979
- [ ] *ABC's of Dance Terminology*, 1949
- [ ] *All-Star Swing Festival* [videorecording], 1972
- [ ] *America Dancing: The Background and Personalities of the Modern Dance*, 1968
- [ ] *American Indian Dances: Steps, Rhythms, Costumes, and Interpretation*, 1963
- [ ] *Around the World in Dance: A New Collection of Folk Dances for Early Childhood* [sound recording], 1972
- [ ] *The Art of the Dance in the U.S.S.R.*, 1968
- [ ] *Ballet and Modern Dance: A Concise History*, 1986
- [ ] *Beginning Social Dance*, 1964
- [ ] *Betty White's Teen-Age Dancebook*, 1963
- [ ] *Black Dance from 1619 to Today*, 1988
- [ ] *Christy Lane's Fun and Funky Freestyle Dancing: Kids, Teens and Adults Sections* [videorecording], 1990
- [ ] *Close Dancing with Donny and Marie: A Step-by-Step Guide to Ballroom Dancing*, 1979

- [ ] *The Complete Guide to Modern Dance*, 1976
- [ ] *Dance! A Complete Guide to Social, Folk and Square Dancing*, 1963
- [ ] *Dance a While: Handbook of Folk, Square, and Social Dance*, 1964
- [ ] *Dance Auditions: Preparations, Presentation, Career Planning*, 1984
- [ ] *Dance Technology: Current Applications and Future Trends*, 1989
- [ ] *Dancing and Dancers of Today: The Modern Revival of Dancing as an Art*, 1978
- [ ] *Dancing as a Career for Men*, 1981
- [ ] *The Fred Astaire Dance Book*, 1978
- [ ] *Let's Dance: Social, Ballroom and Folk Dancing*, 1978
- [ ] *Square Dances of Today and How to Teach and Call Them*, 1950
- [ ] *Teen-Age Dance Etiquette*, 1956
- [ ] *Young Dancer's Career Book*, 1958

796
Sports

GENERAL WEEDING GUIDELINES

700s
5 to 10 years

Biography
5 to 10 years

Fiction
5 to 15 years

Short Stories
5 to 15 years

Why Weed Sports?

Titles with sports and sports figures as a theme are especially important to K–12 library media collections in attracting reluctant readers. To convert those reluctant readers to lifelong readers, you have to provide reading materials that will first attract them, then hold their interest, and finally make them want to come back for more. Readers who are disappointed with materials that are out of date and unattractive will be even more reluctant to continue reading.

Dewey Numbers to Check

Most of your sports books will be in the 796s (Athletic and Outdoor Sports and Games). Check the biography section (both individual and collective) for titles on sports personalities. Review the fiction titles and any short story collections with a sports theme. The reference and AV collections should be checked also.

Specific Criteria for Weeding

The following criteria are very important in weeding sports: accuracy, appearance, bias, and timeliness. Accuracy is important because many students who love sports—but perhaps not school or reading—may be experts on sports information and statistics. Your collection as a whole loses credibility with these students when they recognize inaccuracies. The physical appearance of sports titles must also be considered. Any popular sports title will show wear and tear, so when a title looks bad, replace it with a new copy if it's still in print. Any title that is older than ten years but still in mint physical shape is probably an item that the students are not interested in. Bias in sports materials is often gender-based but sometimes may be racially related. Be careful in keeping older titles directed specifically toward girls or boys. As for timeliness, sports histories are fine if presented as history. However, if the title includes *modern* or *today*, make sure the material is current. Otherwise, discard it.

Tips for Replacing Titles

Sports activities are increasingly unisex. Purchase titles so your collection reflects this trend.

Consider Weeding Titles Like These

- [ ] *100 Greatest Sports Heroes*, 1954
- [ ] *100 Greatest Women in Sports*, 1976
- [ ] *The American Girl Book of Sports Stories*, 1949
- [ ] *The Art of Officiating Sports*, 1957
- [ ] *Baseball Players Do Amazing Things*, 1972
- [ ] *Better Basketball for Boys*, 1960
- [ ] *Bikes: A How-to-Do-It Guide to Selection, Care, Repair, Maintenance, Decoration, Safety, and Fun on Your Bicycle*, 1972
- [ ] *Careers in Sports*, 1975
- [ ] *Famous American Athletes of Today*, 1937
- [ ] *Hammond's Sports Atlas of America: A Guide to Good Fishing, Hunting, and Other Outdoor Sports in the United States and Canada*, 1956
- [ ] *Intramural and Recreational Sports for High School and College*, 1958
- [ ] *Karting: Fun on Four Wheels*, 1975
- [ ] *Meet the Infielders*, 1977
- [ ] *The Negro in Sports*, 1949
- [ ] *Official Rules of Sports and Games*, 1954
- [ ] *Pictorial History of American Sports: From Colonial Times to the Present*, 1952
- [ ] *Roller Skating Is for Me*, 1981
- [ ] *Sport Stories for Boys*, 1956
- [ ] *Sports Injuries Manual for Trainers and Coaches*, 1956
- [ ] *Team Sports for Girls*, 1958
- [ ] *Terry Bradshaw: Superarm of Pro Football*, 1976
- [ ] *Tips from the Top: 52 Golf Lessons by the Country's Leading Pros*, 1955
- [ ] *Walt Frazier: No. 1 Guard of the NBA*, 1976
- [ ] *Wrestling Is for Me*, 1979

796.357
Baseball

GENERAL WEEDING GUIDELINES

700s
5 to 10 years

Biography
5 to 10 years

Fiction
5 to 15 years

Why Weed Baseball?

"Baseball, mom, and apple pie." "The national pastime." Fans or not, everybody seems to accept the place of baseball in the cultural history of America. Students today may have a different approach to the sport—selecting their trading cards on the Web instead of random chance with chewing gum packs, and competing in Internet fantasy baseball leagues instead of at the local lot. Is your collection updated enough to attract their interest?

Dewey Numbers to Check

Most titles will be in the 796.357s (Baseball). Review biographies classed here as well as those in the individual and collective sections. Try to review those fiction titles that you can find with a central theme of baseball. The reference collection may have a few record books to review, but be sure to check the AV collection also.

Specific Criteria for Weeding

Nonfiction baseball titles should be accurate, attractive, and up to date. This area presents an opportunity to draw in reluctant readers because of their interest in sports, so keeping old and boring titles on the shelf will do more harm than good, even if there is a golden nugget of information between the covers. Your users will be ruthless here so be sure you are as well when weeding. While reviewing content, watch for signs of gender and race bias—sometimes blatantly in the title, at other times more subtly in the illustrations.

Fiction titles with a theme of baseball will be harder to locate on the fiction shelves since they are so scattered, but search for those that are hopelessly out of touch with students of today. There are lots of new titles on the market that will encourage reading and maybe even inspire your students to experience that American "joy in Mudville."

Tips for Replacing Titles

Interest in some baseball subjects will be fueled by current events. The stem cell research issue may stimulate student interest in Lou Gehrig and prompt you to update his biography. Past baseball scandals ("say it ain't so, Joe") could use refreshing when new information is available. Ted Williams biographies should be updated to reflect his death and also the cryonics afterlife controversy. The use of steroids is drumming up both interest and controversy.

Consider Weeding Titles Like These

- [ ] *100 Greatest Baseball Heroes*, 1974
- [ ] *All-Star Baseball since 1933*, 1980
- [ ] *The Baseball Encyclopedia: The Complete and Official Record of Major League Baseball*, 1976
- [ ] *Baseball for Boys*, 1960
- [ ] *Baseball's Greatest All-Star Games*, 1979
- [ ] *Baseball's Greatest Players Today*, 1963
- [ ] *Baseball's Most Valuable Players*, 1966
- [ ] *Careers in Baseball*, 1973
- [ ] *Complete Guide to Baseball Slang*, 1980
- [ ] *The Great American Baseball Card Flipping, Trading, and Bubble Gum Book*, 1973
- [ ] *Great Baseball Stories: Today and Yesterday*, 1978
- [ ] *Great No-Hit Games of the Major Leagues*, 1968
- [ ] *How to Play Big League Baseball: Complete Playing Instructions for Every Position*, 1951
- [ ] *How to Star in Baseball*, 1960
- [ ] *Modern Baseball Superstars*, 1973
- [ ] *More Modern Baseball Superstars*, 1978
- [ ] *New Breed Heroes in Pro Baseball*, 1974
- [ ] *Rookie of the Year* [videorecording], 1972
- [ ] *Something Queer at the Ballpark: A Mystery*, 1975
- [ ] *Stars of the Series: A Complete History of the World Series*, 1964
- [ ] *There've Been Some Changes in the World of Sports*, 1962
- [ ] *Trade Him! 100 Years of Baseball's Greatest Deals*, 1976
- [ ] *What a Baseball Manager Does*, 1970
- [ ] *A Wife's Guide to Baseball*, 1970
- [ ] *The World Series: A Complete Pictorial History*, 1976

796.48
Olympic Games

GENERAL WEEDING
GUIDELINES

700s
5 to 10 years

Biography
5 to 10 years

Why Weed the Olympic Games?

The modern Olympic Games are accompanied by a media blitz. The publishing world also seems to participate in this cycle by releasing many new titles after each Olympics. Take advantage of the timing to purchase the best of the titles available after each and to weed your collection on this subject.

Dewey Numbers to Check

Most titles on the Olympics will be found in the 796s: 796.48 for the summer games and 796.98 for the winter games. In addition, you will probably have both individual and collective biographies that should be reviewed. Also check the reference and AV collections.

Specific Criteria for Weeding

Although it may be fine to keep older titles for specific Olympic Games, it is not good to keep general histories of the games that imply they are up to date but were published in the 1970s, 1980s, or even the 1990s. Let the title as well as the content be your guide. Older general titles will not have some topics of interest to students today such as the IOC (International Olympic Committee) position on professional athletes (1981), the beginning of steroid use and testing (1988), the Dream Team (1992), or the Tonya/Nancy saga (1994).

With biographies, pay close attention to personalities as well as content. In the case of Jim Thorpe, any biography published before 1982 (when his medals were restored) is outdated. Athletes who were popular twenty or thirty years ago may have faded from public interest—replace their biographies with those of more current Olympic personalities. Some older Olympic athletes may still be in the public eye, but students today may associate them with pain medication advertisements instead of Wheaties boxes. If you still need titles on them, weed and update.

Tips for Replacing Titles

Always add titles for the most recently completed games, but also update older games as needed. When new titles come out for a past specific Olympics, it is probably because new information is now available on a controversy or an event associated with it.

Consider Weeding Titles Like These

- [ ] *After Olympic Glory: The Lives of Ten Outstanding Medalists*, 1978
- [ ] *Bruce Jenner's Guide to the Olympics*, 1979
- [ ] *The Complete Book of the Olympics*, 1988
- [ ] *Encyclopedia of the Olympic Games*, 1972
- [ ] *The First Book of the Olympic Games*, 1971
- [ ] *Getting into Olympic Form: Those Who Know Tell What It Takes*, 1980
- [ ] *Golden Girls: True Stories of Olympic Women Stars*, 1980
- [ ] *Goofy Presents the Olympics: A Fun and Exciting History of the Olympics from the Ancient Games to Today*, 1979
- [ ] *The Greatest Moments in Olympic History* [videorecording], 1987
- [ ] *Highlights of the Olympics from Ancient Times to the Present*, 1969
- [ ] *Jim Thorpe: All-Around Athlete*, 1971
- [ ] *Mary Lou Retton and the New Gymnasts*, 1985
- [ ] *The Modern Olympics*, 1976
- [ ] *Olympic Controversies*, 1987
- [ ] *The Olympic Fun Fact Book*, 1988
- [ ] *The Olympic Games*, 1976
- [ ] *The Olympic Games Handbook: An Authentic History of Both the Ancient and Modern Olympic Games, Complete Results and Records*, 1975
- [ ] *A Political History of the Olympic Games*, 1981
- [ ] *Stars of the Modern Olympics*, 1967
- [ ] *Stories from the Olympics: From 776 B.C. to Now*, 1976
- [ ] *The Summer Olympics*, 1979
- [ ] *Timetables of Sports History: The Olympic Games*, 1990
- [ ] *The Winter Olympics*, 1979
- [ ] *Women Gold Medal Winners* [videorecording], 1975
- [ ] *Young Olympic Champions*, 1973

808
Poetry

Why Weed Poetry?

If weeding is the most neglected duty in a busy library media center, then the poetry section is probably the most ignored weeding area in even a well-tended collection. Review this gentle section and offer an attractive collection of poetry for your students.

Dewey Numbers to Check

Many poetry anthologies will be found classed in the general 808s (Rhetoric and Collections of Literary Texts from More Than Two Literatures). Review the remainder of the 800 section for poetry collections based on a single language: 811 (American Poetry), 821 (English Poetry), 831 (German Poetry), 841 (French Poetry), and so on. Check the reference and the AV collections also.

Specific Criteria for Weeding

Before you start looking at individual titles in the poetry section, stand back and take a general look at the area. Is there any eye appeal to attract students? If not, this area will be visited only for classroom assignments. Increase the appeal of this section (and the valuable older indexed titles that you keep) by adding a few of the new and attractive titles on the market today. Some of those older titles should be weeded and replaced if they are in bad physical condition or if they are misleading to your students.

   The term *modern* may be acceptable in titles if the implication is literary rather than present day. But titles that do imply currency should be carefully evaluated. Some older titles may also have an ethnic or a gender bias that could be offensive. The AV collection probably has some old titles in formats such as filmstrips or vinyl records that should be discarded.

Tips for Replacing Titles

Order titles that will build up the national sections to reflect the global awareness and diversity of students today.

Consider Weeding Titles Like These

- [ ] *31 New American Poets*, 1969
- [ ] *All Things New: An Anthology*, 1965
- [ ] *American Poets: From the Puritans to the Present*, 1968
- [ ] *Anthology of Contemporary American Poetry* [sound recording], 1962
- [ ] *An Anthology of Irish Verse: The Poetry of Ireland from Mythological Times to the Present*, 1948
- [ ] *Anthology of Korean Poetry: From the Earliest Era to the Present*, 1964
- [ ] *An Anthology of Modern Hebrew Poetry*, 1968
- [ ] *An Anthology of the New England Poets from Colonial Times to the Present Day*, 1948
- [ ] *Black Out Loud: An Anthology of Modern Poems by Black Americans*, 1970
- [ ] *Con Cuba: An Anthology of Cuban Poetry of the Last Sixty Years*, 1969
- [ ] *Contemporary American Poets: American Poetry since 1940*, 1969
- [ ] *Ebony Rhythm: An Anthology of Contemporary Negro Verse*, 1968
- [ ] *Fifteen Modern American Poets*, 1956
- [ ] *Gaily We Parade: A Collection of Poems about People, Here, There, and Everywhere*, 1940
- [ ] *How to Read and Understand Poetry* [filmstrip], 1966
- [ ] *Images of Tomorrow: An Anthology of Recent Poetry*, 1953
- [ ] *New American and Canadian Poetry*, 1971
- [ ] *A New Anthology of Modern Poetry*, 1946
- [ ] *The New Modern Poetry: British and American Poetry since World War II*, 1967
- [ ] *The New Pocket Anthology of American Verse from Colonial Days to the Present*, 1955
- [ ] *Parachutes Could Carry Us Higher: Poems about Today*, 1972
- [ ] *Poems by Contemporary Women*, 1979
- [ ] *Poems for Modern Youth*, 1938
- [ ] *Visions of America: By the Poets of Our Time*, 1968
- [ ] *Voices of the Rainbow: Contemporary Poetry by American Indians*, 1975

808.7
Wit and Humor

Why Weed Wit and Humor?

Knock, knock.
Who's there?
Dewey.
Dewey who?
Dewey have to weed wit and humor?
Yes! Your students will be very happy if you update this much-used and much-loved section of the library!

Dewey Numbers to Check

Most general titles will be found at 808.7 (Rhetoric of Humor and Satire). Also scan various national approaches in 817 (American Humor and Satire in English), 827 (English Humor and Satire), and so on through the 800s and the various languages. Do a quick check if you have time, but your reference section is most likely missing wit and humor. Humor may be found in the AV collection, however, so check there.

Specific Criteria for Weeding

A well-loved book of jokes leads a hard life. Replace titles when the condition demands. Find out if some of these old titles have been reprinted recently—this is a good sign that the humor included has staying power with today's students. Review all titles to see if they have a gender or nationality bias that you want to avoid in your collection today. Also, some topics from years ago might be outdated in interest as well as sensitivity. Look at the illustrations as well as the text to determine the message sent by the humor.

Tips for Replacing Titles

Don't be overly concerned about the age and grade levels when purchasing wit and humor titles. You can bend a little and purchase at a lower level than you usually do for most topics. Your students won't be insulted. Even adults tend to enjoy some humor at a grade level more like their shoe size instead of their age! Relax and laugh.

Consider Weeding Titles Like These

- [ ] *500 Best Irish Jokes and Limericks*, 1970
- [ ] *1,000 Jokes for Kids of All Ages*, 1974
- [ ] *2,000 Insults for All Occasions*, 1977
- [ ] *2,000 New Laughs for Speakers: The Ad-libber's Handbook*, 1969
- [ ] *American Humor and Whimsy* [filmstrip], 1978
- [ ] *Anything for a Laugh: A Collection of Jokes and Anecdotes that You, Too, Can Tell and Probably Have*, 1946
- [ ] *Asian Laughter: An Anthology of Oriental Satire and Humor*, 1971
- [ ] *Bennett Cerf's Bumper Crop of Anecdotes and Stories, Mostly Humorous, about the Famous and Near Famous*, 1959
- [ ] *The Book of Negro Humor*, 1966
- [ ] *A Carnival of Modern Humor*, 1967
- [ ] *Encyclopedia of Black Folklore and Humor*, 1972
- [ ] *Encyclopedia of Jewish Humor: From Biblical Times to the Modern Age*, 1969
- [ ] *An Encyclopedia of Modern American Humor*, 1954
- [ ] *Gag Galaxy: Outer Space Jokes and Riddles*, 1980
- [ ] *Holy Laughter: Essays on Religion in the Comic Perspective*, 1969
- [ ] *The Home Book of Irish Humor*, 1968
- [ ] *Knock Knocks You've Never Heard Before*, 1977
- [ ] *The Life of the Party: A New Collection of Stories and Anecdotes*, 1956
- [ ] *The Modern Handbook of Humor*, 1967
- [ ] *Podium Humor: A Raconteur's Treasury of Witty and Humorous Stories*, 1975
- [ ] *Shake Well Before Using: A New Collection of Impressions and Anecdotes, Mostly Humorous*, 1948
- [ ] *Space Out! Jokes about Outer Space*, 1984
- [ ] *Speaker's Encyclopedia of Humor: Stories, Quotes, Definitions, and Toasts for Every Situation*, 1961
- [ ] *Teen-Age Treasury of Good Humor*, 1960
- [ ] *Toaster's Handbook: Jokes, Stories, and Quotations*, 1938

822.3
Shakespeare

Why Weed Shakespeare?

William Shakespeare lived and wrote some four hundred years ago in England, but his many works live on in school library media collections worldwide. Many of those titles by and about Shakespeare are physically old and unattractive, a shame since the publishing world releases wonderful new titles each year. Update your collection and spark a new interest in Shakespeare!

Dewey Numbers to Check

Almost all the works by Shakespeare will be found at 822.3 (William Shakespeare)—his own Dewey number under English drama! Check your biographies of Shakespeare as well as the reference and AV collections.

Specific Criteria for Weeding

First look at the appearance and physical condition of the titles in the 822.3s. Replace worn-out titles with newer editions (if available) or alternate new titles. For those older titles that are still in good shape but don't appear to be circulating, decide if it is the presentation or the subject matter that is keeping them on the shelf and weed accordingly. But be safe and check with your English teachers before removing these titles from the collection so you won't be caught short for an upcoming classroom assignment.

Don't consult or debate about old filmstrips or videorecordings. Replace with new titles that have received positive reviews. Offer weeded AV titles to the English department if you feel it necessary, but remove them from the library collection.

Tips for Replacing Titles

Controversies over the life and writings of Shakespeare have been around for years. If you stock any of these titles, keep only the most recent. The others are old news easily discounted by the popular press and the Internet. Also, investigate downloadable audiobooks of some of Shakespeare's works for this MP3 generation!

Consider Weeding Titles Like These

- [ ] *An Approach to Shakespeare*, 1956
- [ ] *An Authenticated Contemporary Portrait of Shakespeare*, 1932
- [ ] *Character and Motive in Shakespeare: Some Recent Appraisals Examined*, 1966
- [ ] *A Complete View of the Shakespeare Controversy, Concerning the Authenticity and Genuineness of Manuscript Matter Affecting the Works and Biography of Shakespeare*, 1973
- [ ] *The Design Within: Psychoanalytic Approaches to Shakespeare*, 1970
- [ ] *Directing Shakespeare in the Contemporary Theatre*, 1974
- [ ] *The Genius of Shakespeare* [filmstrip], 1969
- [ ] *Life in Elizabethan Times* [filmstrip], 1958
- [ ] *Multi-media Shakespeare* [filmstrip], 1971
- [ ] *A New and Complete Concordance or Verbal Index to Words, Phrases, and Passages in the Dramatic Works of Shakespeare, with a Supplementary Concordance to the Poems*, 1972
- [ ] *A New Companion to Shakespeare Studies*, 1971
- [ ] *Presenting William Shakespeare* [video-recording], 1975
- [ ] *Recent Discoveries Relating to the Life and Works of William Shakespeare*, 1973
- [ ] *Selected Shakespearean Tragedies: Plots and Analyses* [filmstrip], 1965
- [ ] *Shakespeare and His Rivals: A Casebook on the Authorship Controversy*, 1962
- [ ] *The Shakespeare Claimants: A Critical Survey of the Four Principal Theories Concerning the Authorship of the Shakespearean Plays*, 1962
- [ ] *Shakespeare: Contemporary Critical Approaches*, 1980
- [ ] *Shakespeare: Mirror of a Man* [filmstrip], 1969
- [ ] *Shakespeare: Modern Essays in Criticism*, 1957
- [ ] *Shakespeare's Plays Today: Some Customs and Conventions of the Stage*, 1971
- [ ] *Understanding Shakespeare*, 1962
- [ ] *Was Shakespeare Shakespeare? A Lawyer Reviews the Evidence*, 1965
- [ ] *Wasn't Shakespeare Someone Else? New Evidence in the Very Words of the Bard Himself about His True Identity*, 1971
- [ ] *Who Was Shakespeare? A New Enquiry*, 1970
- [ ] *Who Was Shakespeare? The Man, the Times, the Works*, 1974

910
Geography

Why Weed Geography?

We've all seen it in the newspapers and heard it on the news: Many students in the United States today lack basic knowledge of geography. Too many of our students are unable to find their own state on a map of the United States or locate a major world feature such as the Persian Gulf. In today's global world, students must become more knowledgeable about geography. Make sure your collection gives them current information in an attractive format.

Dewey Numbers to Check

The 910s (Geography and Travel) are your target to review for this topic. Check the reference section as well as the circulating collection. This topic also has many AV titles in K–12 collections, so review that area.

Specific Criteria for Weeding

Political geography titles should be changed as often as the political boundaries or names of those countries and regions change. Physical geography titles have a longer shelf life but need to be reviewed to see if the information is presented in an attractive and appealing format. Elementary collections will have the most titles on general geography, but all K–12 levels should have current titles on specific countries. Especially look for countries currently in the news to make sure you are providing updated information. The publishing market always follows important news events, so you will be able to find new titles to replace the outdated ones.

Books emphasizing travel must be very current to be at all useful. Discard old titles and purchase new ones only for those countries that you can keep updated.

Tips for Replacing Titles

Apply the same standards for books and AV titles to any globes and wall maps in your center and update as needed.

Consider Weeding Titles Like These

- ☐ *Africa: A Social, Economic, and Political Geography of Its Major Regions*, 1967
- ☐ *Asia's Land and Peoples: A Geography of One-Third of the Earth and Two-Thirds of Its People*, 1963
- ☐ *Countries of the World*, 1978
- ☐ *East-Central Europe: An Introductory Geography*, 1967
- ☐ *Emerging Africa: An Introduction to the History, Geography, Peoples, and Current Problems of the Multi-national African Continent on Its Way from Colonialism to Independence*, 1969
- ☐ *Encyclopedia of World Geography: Man and His World Today*, 1974
- ☐ *The First Golden Book of Geography: A Beginner's Introduction to Our World*, 1955
- ☐ *Flags of All Nations and the People Who Live Under Them*, 1967
- ☐ *Geography Can Be Fun*, 1951
- ☐ *Geography of Europe*, 1965
- ☐ *Geography of U.S.S.R.*, 1964
- ☐ *Germany: An Introductory Geography*, 1968
- ☐ *The Golden Geography: A Child's Introduction to the World*, 1952

- ☐ *Illustrated Atlas for Young America: Full-Color Maps and Up-to-Date Facts with New Concepts about Our Physical and Political World*, 1967
- ☐ *The Land around Us: Concepts in Geography* [filmstrip], 1976
- ☐ *Land of the 500 Million: A Geography of China*, 1955
- ☐ *A Modern Geography of the United States: Aspects of Life and Economy*, 1972
- ☐ *Our Dynamic World: A Survey in Modern Geography*, 1966
- ☐ *Our Geography: Why Cultures Are Different* [filmstrip], 1974
- ☐ *An Outline of Political Geography*, 1942
- ☐ *People and Geography of South America* [filmstrip], 1972
- ☐ *Picture Map Geography of Africa*, 1964
- ☐ *The World Today: A Fascinating Book about People and Places*, 1969
- ☐ *The World Today: Its Patterns and Cultures*, 1963
- ☐ *Worlds without End: Exploration from 2000 B.C. to Today*, 1956

920
Biography

Why Weed Biography?

It's easy to bypass the biography sections when weeding a collection. After all, a good number of biographies in school libraries are on historical figures long since dead. But current developments and research often change our perception of historical as well as contemporary figures. And a title that was chosen for its contemporary value years ago may have little meaning or interest for today's students.

Dewey Numbers to Check

Start with the 920s (Biography, Genealogy, Insignia). Most K–12 libraries, however, have elected to keep their collective biographies (brief biographies about several people in one book) in the 920s and their individual biographies and autobiographies in another area, usually designated with a B or 92 and arranged alphabetically according to the last name of the subject of the biography (or autobiography). If a collective biography title is all about people in the same subject area, it will probably be classed and shelved with that subject (for example, sports figures in the 796s). Also check the reference and AV collections.

Specific Criteria for Weeding

Review biography titles with particular attention to gender and race bias, changes in perception over time, and currency of interest. Look at collective biographies with titles that imply only men had an impact on the development of science, medicine, or politics while women were change agents only in such fields as nursing. Titles that target the achievements of racial or gender groups must also be checked for sensitivity.

Look for titles on personalities (such as Pete Rose or Richard Nixon) whose public perception has changed because of personal or historical issues. When major news stories come out about figures in your collection, put those names on your watch list and be prepared to replace the biographies when new ones are published.

Tips for Replacing Titles

To stimulate interest, build up your biography collection with some contemporary figures. But be prepared to weed these biographies when interest fades, especially those of popular music or other celebrities.

Consider Weeding Titles Like These

- [ ] *The 100 Greatest Baseball Players of All Time*, 1986
- [ ] *America's Twelve Great Women Leaders during the Past Hundred Years as Chosen by the Women of America*, 1969
- [ ] *American Composers: A Study of the Music of This Country and of Its Future, with Biographies of the Leading Composers of the Present Time*, 1973
- [ ] *The Best of the Music Makers: From Acuff to Ellington to Presley to Sinatra to Zappa and 279 More of the Most Popular Performers of the Last Fifty Years*, 1979
- [ ] *Bjorn Borg: The Coolest Ace*, 1979
- [ ] *Carol Heiss: Olympic Queen*, 1961
- [ ] *Champions of the Bat: Baseball's Greatest Sluggers*, 1967
- [ ] *Contemporary American Indian Leaders*, 1972
- [ ] *Contributions of Women: Politics and Government*, 1977
- [ ] *Coretta King: A Woman of Peace*, 1974
- [ ] *Daredevils of the Speedway*, 1966
- [ ] *Donahue: My Own Story*, 1979
- [ ] *Donny and Marie Osmond: Breaking All the Rules*, 1977
- [ ] *The Ebony Book of Black Achievement*, 1970
- [ ] *Famous American Musicians*, 1972
- [ ] *The Films of Steve McQueen*, 1978

- [ ] *Gerald Ford and the Future of the Presidency*, 1974
- [ ] *The Great Singers: From the Dawn of Opera to Our Own Time*, 1966
- [ ] *The Greatest in Sports: All Time Heroes of Baseball, Football, and Track*, 1972
- [ ] *Happy Trails: The Story of Roy Rogers and Dale Evans*, 1979
- [ ] *Heroes of Our Time*, 1962
- [ ] *I Didn't Do It Alone: The Autobiography of Art Linkletter*, 1980
- [ ] *I'm Gonna Make You Love Me: The Story of Diana Ross*, 1980
- [ ] *An Intimate Close-Up of America's First Family*, 1977
- [ ] *Lawrence Welk: Champagne Music Man*, 1968
- [ ] *Living Musicians*, 1964
- [ ] *Modern Americans in Science and Invention*, 1941
- [ ] *Ms. Africa: Profiles of Modern African Women*, 1973
- [ ] *Singing Sweetly: Cher, Roberta Flack, Olivia Newton John*, 1976
- [ ] *Superstars of Golf*, 1978
- [ ] *The Superstars of Rock: Their Lives and Their Music*, 1980
- [ ] *Superstars of Sports: Today and Yesterday*, 1978
- [ ] *Twenty Modern Americans*, 1942

940
Europe

Why Weed Europe?

Europe (both Eastern and Western) has undergone numerous political, social, cultural, and geographical changes in the past twenty years. New constitutions have been written, some countries have divided, others have united, many countries have changed. School media center collections may still own titles for countries that no longer exist or are now drastically different from their earlier forms. Review and update so your collection is not guilty of giving out-of-date information on this area.

Dewey Numbers to Check

Start at 940 (History of Europe), but you will be checking all of the 940s from 941 (British Isles) to 949.9 (Bulgaria). Check the reference and AV collections also.

Specific Criteria for Weeding

Although the unification of Germany in 1989 is a good example of a major European country change, it is just one of many. The former countries of Czechoslovakia, Yugoslavia, and the Soviet Union have all experienced important transformations. Political systems in Eastern Europe have changed from Communist-controlled states to elected governments. New solutions such as an economic union and a shared currency have spread across most of Europe. New ethnic problems and immigration problems preoccupy many European countries. Cultural change and a rapidly decreasing population are also common to most European countries. Older titles will include none of these important current issues. Reconsider any history of a country in Europe if it does not bring students up to the current situation.

Resist the urge to move outdated travel books to the history section. They are still out of date and should be weeded.

Tips for Replacing Titles

If you have doubts about a print or an AV item and are wondering if the country still exists in the same form, a quick online check of the World Factbook (http://www.cia.gov) will give you fast information that is concise, reliable, and current. If the title in question is found to be out of date, you should be able to find a replacement title on the market.

Consider Weeding Titles Like These

- [ ] *Behind the Iron Curtain: The Soviet Satellite States*, 1964
- [ ] *Camping Guide to Europe: The Most Inexpensive Way to Tour the Continent*, 1968
- [ ] *Come Along to East Germany*, 1969
- [ ] *Communism in Eastern Europe*, 1979
- [ ] *Discovery Trips in Europe*, 1972
- [ ] *Eastern Europe, A to Z: Bulgaria, Czechoslovakia, East Germany, Hungary, Poland, Romania, Yugoslavia and the Soviet Union*, 1968
- [ ] *Eastern Europe after Czechoslovakia*, 1969
- [ ] *Europe and America: The Next Ten Years*, 1970
- [ ] *Europe and the Modern World*, 1969
- [ ] *Europe in Our Time: 1914 to the Present*, 1948
- [ ] *Europe Now: A First Hand Report*, 1945
- [ ] *Festivals in Europe*, 1954
- [ ] *Fun in Europe: The Cosmopolitan Traveler's Grand Tour of the Continent*, 1959
- [ ] *Geography of Europe* [filmstrip], 1982
- [ ] *Germany: East and West*, 1968
- [ ] *Get Ready! Get Set! Go! A European Travel Guide for Young People*, 1970
- [ ] *Getting to Know the Two Germanys*, 1966
- [ ] *Grand European Itineraries: Everything You Need to Know to Plan Your Own Memorable Vacation*, 1987
- [ ] *Guide to Study in Europe: A Selective Guide to European Schools and Universities*, 1969
- [ ] *How to Get to Europe and Have a Wonderful Time: A Consumer's Handbook on Travel*, 1971
- [ ] *Inside Europe Today*, 1962
- [ ] *Modern Political Systems: Europe*, 1968
- [ ] *New Governments in Europe: The Trend toward Dictatorship*, 1970
- [ ] *Seeing Eastern Europe* [filmstrip], 1963
- [ ] *So You're Going to Germany and Austria! And if I Were Going with You These Are the Things I'd Invite You to Do*, 1936

940.53
The Holocaust

Why Weed the Holocaust?

Recent reports of increased racism and religious intolerance—especially in Europe—are of concern worldwide. Perhaps the time is right to review and update your titles on the Holocaust to make sure our students are learning from history and not doomed to repeat it.

GENERAL WEEDING GUIDELINES

900s
5 to 15 years

Biography
5 to 10 years

Fiction
5 to 15 years

Dewey Numbers to Check

Holocaust titles are located at 940.53 (World War II, 1939–1945), but this includes all the Holocaust years of 1933–1945. You may want to check 362.87 (Victims of Oppression) to see if you have any older titles still at that former location for the Holocaust. The reference, AV, and biography sections should be reviewed—especially Anne Frank biography titles. Since this is a topic that crosses over to the fiction section also, review low-circulating titles with the Holocaust as a theme and replace with new, high-interest ones.

Specific Criteria for Weeding

Approach weeding the Holocaust section with three objectives in mind: preserving primary source materials, updating facts and perspectives on that time in history, and providing materials that have appeal to today's students. Titles with primary source information should be retained if they are still physically acceptable. If physical condition is a problem, replace with newer editions when available or provide the protection of circulation limits or a change of physical housing. Offer a balance on popular-press Holocaust denial by providing information so students can see those current claims against past documented histories.

Tips for Replacing Titles

Anne Frank is a name that personifies this time. Update her biography to a newer version that more closely follows her diary instead of the earlier editions that were heavily edited by her father. Watch for an updated biography on the life of Simon Wiesenthal. Also consider adding some of the graphic novels available on the Holocaust.

Consider Weeding Titles Like These

- *Anne Frank: A Legacy for Our Time* [filmstrip], 1985
- *Anne Frank: The Diary of a Young Girl*, 1960
- *Anthology of Holocaust Literature*, 1978
- *Anti-Semitism in Europe: Sources of the Holocaust*, 1976
- *Anti-Semitism: The Road to the Holocaust and Beyond*, 1982
- *Approaches to Auschwitz: The Holocaust and Its Legacy*, 1986
- *Can It Happen Again? Chronicles of the Holocaust*, 1995
- *Classroom Strategies for Teaching about the Holocaust: 10 Lessons for Classroom Use*, 1983
- *The Cunning of History: Mass Death and the American Future*, 1975
- *The Encyclopedia of the Holocaust*, 1990
- *Fifty Years Ago: In the Depths of Darkness; Commemoration Planning Guide*, 1991
- *History of the Holocaust: A Handbook and Dictionary*, 1994
- *The Holocaust* [filmstrip], 1977
- *The Holocaust: An Annotated Bibliography and Resource Guide*, 1985
- *The Holocaust in Historical Perspective*, 1978
- *The Jewish Return into History: Reflections in the Age of Auschwitz and a New Jerusalem*, 1978
- *"My Brother's Keeper?" Recent Polish Debates on the Holocaust*, 1990
- *Out of the Holocaust* [filmstrip], 1974
- *Preserving the Past to Ensure the Future* [videorecording], 1990
- *Simon Wiesenthal: A Life in Search of Justice*, 1996
- *A Time to Remember: A Modern Overview of the Holocaust* [videorecording], 1980
- *A Tree Still Stands: Jewish Youth in Eastern Europe Today*, 1990
- *Unanswered Questions: Nazi Germany and the Genocide of the Jews*, 1989
- *Understanding the Holocaust*, 1982

940.53
World War II

Why Weed World War II?

The year 2005 marked the sixtieth anniversary of the end of World War II (WWII) and the first anniversary of the World War II Memorial in Washington, D.C. Recognizing that fewer than 5 million U.S. veterans now survive of the more than 16 million who served in those war years, a flurry of commemorative events, educational activities, and publishing is currently taking place. There are wonderful new and interesting titles available now to supplement or replace aging titles in school library collections.

Dewey Numbers to Check

Check 940.53 (World War II, 1939–1945) and 940.54 (Military History of World War II). It's especially important to review your AV and reference collections also because of the number of new AV titles and reference resources recently released. There may be some titles in the biography sections that should be updated.

Specific Criteria for Weeding

As with any historical event, save any primary source materials that are still appropriate for the collection but reconsider titles that deal with interpretation and controversies that might have changed over the years. Don't keep postwar accounts of countries involved in the war that are misleading about the current state of those countries. Be wary of keeping WWII encyclopedias that are old, especially if they are located in the reference collection. Although older AV titles may have the same archival photographs as newer titles, the replacement titles will likely include enhanced photographs as well as reenactments and may include contrasting current views of those past locations in order to make the events more interesting to students today.

Tips for Replacing Titles

Replace any borderline print or AV titles with some of the attractive new titles on the market now.

Consider Weeding Titles Like These

- [ ] *After Victory: Churchill, Roosevelt, Stalin and the Making of the Peace*, 1967
- [ ] *British and American Tanks of World War II: The Complete Illustrated History of British, American and Commonwealth Tanks, Gun Motor Carriages and Special Purpose Vehicles*, 1969
- [ ] *The Brutal Friendship: Mussolini, Hitler, and the Fall of Italian Fascism*, 1962
- [ ] *Burn after Reading: The Espionage History of World War II*, 1961
- [ ] *Captains without Eyes: Intelligence Failures in World War II*, 1969
- [ ] *The Case against Adolf Eichmann*, 1960
- [ ] *Causes of World War II* [filmstrip], 1970
- [ ] *Churchill, Roosevelt, Stalin: The War They Waged and the Peace They Sought*, 1957
- [ ] *The Complete History of World War II*, 1949
- [ ] *Double-Edged Secrets: U.S. Naval Intelligence Operations in the Pacific during World War II*, 1979
- [ ] *The End of Glory: An Interpretation of the Origin of World War II*, 1970
- [ ] *The Game of the Foxes: The Untold Story of German Espionage in the United States and Great Britain during World War II*, 1971
- [ ] *Hitler's Spies: German Military Intelligence in World War II*, 1978
- [ ] *Illustrated World War II Encyclopedia: An Unbiased Account of the Most Devastating War Known to Mankind*, 1978
- [ ] *None More Courageous: American War Heroes of Today*, 1942
- [ ] *The Origins of the Cold War, 1941–1947: A Historical Problem with Interpretations and Documents*, 1962
- [ ] *The Outbreak of the Second World War: Design or Blunder?* 1962
- [ ] *The Russian Version of the Second World War: The History of the War as Taught to Soviet School Children*, 1976
- [ ] *The Shadow of Pearl Harbor: Political Controversy over the Surprise Attack, 1941–1946*, 1977
- [ ] *Summary of the Second World War and Its Consequences: An Alphabetical Reference Book; Persons, Places and Events, Scientific and Military Developments, and Postwar Problems in Preserving Peace*, 1947
- [ ] *The Trial of the Germans: An Account of the Twenty-two Defendants before the International Military Tribunal at Nuremberg*, 1966
- [ ] *What Happened at Pearl Harbor?* 1958
- [ ] *When the Saboteurs Came: The Nazi Sabotage Plot against America in World War II*, 1967
- [ ] *The World since 1919*, 1954
- [ ] *World War II* [filmstrip], 1972

947
Russia

Why Weed Russia?

Would your students be confused if they checked out a book (or watched an AV item) from your collection on Russia and then went home to see a news clip on TV of the Russian president riding in a pick-up truck in Texas with a modern U.S. president? Times change. National alliances change. Library media collections must keep up with those changes.

Dewey Numbers to Check

The 947s (Eastern Europe—Russia) will be your target for this topic. Also check the 914.7s (Geography and Travel in Russia). Check both sections in the reference and AV collections.

Specific Criteria for Weeding

Russia, the world's largest country with a history spanning ten centuries, probably is not a large subject section in your media collection. This makes it even more important to have accurate and up-to-date information on this country that has seen dramatic national changes in the past decade. Keep the following Russian timeline dates in mind when you review this section for currency and completeness:

1945–1980s	cold war years
1957	*Sputnik* launch
1962	Cuban missile crisis
1991	U.S.S.R. and state communism era ends, Russian Federation created, and Yeltsin elected first president of Russia
2000	Putin elected president of Russia

The above changes make even history books obsolete if they are older than 1992, unless they are period-specific or primary source works.

Tips for Replacing Titles

Weeding and rebuilding a subject area like this is an ideal opportunity for you to collaborate with your history teachers—but be sure they understand that the purpose of a K–12 library media collection is to have current as well as historical information to support the curriculum.

Consider Weeding Titles Like These

- *Along the Roads of the New Russia*, 1968
- *Basic History of Modern Russia: Political, Cultural, and Social Trends*, 1957
- *Common Sense about Russia*, 1961
- *Communism in the Modern World*, 1962
- *Education and Modernization in the USSR*, 1971
- *Europe and the USSR*, 1960
- *Everyman's Concise Encyclopaedia of Russia*, 1961
- *The Family in Soviet Russia*, 1968
- *Getting to Know the U.S.S.R.*, 1959
- *A History of Russia: Medieval, Modern, and Contemporary*, 1974
- *How People Live in the U.S.S.R.*, 1969
- *How Russia Is Ruled*, 1963
- *Inside Russia Today*, 1962
- *Inside the U.S.S.R.* [filmstrip], 1977
- *Journey across Russia: The Soviet Union Today* [filmstrip], 1977
- *The Land and the People of Russia*, 1966
- *Let's Travel in the Soviet Union*, 1965
- *Life in Russia Today*, 1969
- *Religion in Russia Today*, 1967
- *Russia and Communism* [filmstrip], 1969
- *Russia Re-examined: The Land, the People, and How They Live*, 1967
- *Russia: The Land and People of the Soviet Union*, 1980
- *The Soviet Union: Faces of Today* [video-recording], 1972
- *The USSR Today: Facts and Interpretations*, 1978
- *USSR: Its People, Its Society, Its Culture*, 1960

GENERAL WEEDING GUIDELINES

900s
5 to 15 years

Biography
5 to 10 years

959.7
Vietnam

Why Weed Vietnam?

The Vietnam War continues to stay in the American news. Attention to the still controversial war ebbs and flows over the years, with renewed interest sparked often by some current news event. The conflict in Iraq has resulted in a new examination of Vietnam and the Vietnam War. Make sure your collection offers current information on this country and the war.

Dewey Numbers to Check

Review the 959.7s (Vietnam) for the history of this country, including the Vietnam War of 1961–1975 (959.704). Check 915.97 (Description and Travel) for current accounts of the country. You may also have some titles on the war involvement classed in the U.S. history section 973.92 for that period. Also review the biography, reference, and AV collections.

Specific Criteria for Weeding

As with any historical topic, make sure you keep any primary source or local history titles on the war, but critically review any older titles that imply current analysis or perspective. Keeping the years of the war (1961–1975) in mind, question any war titles published within that time frame. The U.S.-led postwar (1979–1994) embargo against Vietnam and the normalization of relations with the Western world after 1995 should be included in any general history of Vietnam. Check any favorite older title to see if a newer edition has been released. Because many students will be getting their first introduction to Vietnam and the war years via classroom AV presentations, be sure your collection has only current information. Weed and replace those twenty-year-old videorecordings and filmstrips.

Tips for Replacing Titles

Consider adding some fiction titles with Vietnam and the Vietnam War as a theme. New titles are now available.

Consider Weeding Titles Like These

- [ ] *The Air War in Vietnam,* 1968
- [ ] *America in Vietnam* [videorecording], 1980
- [ ] *America on Trial: The War for Vietnam,* 1971
- [ ] *Bringing the War Home: The American Soldier in Vietnam and After,* 1974
- [ ] *Children of Vietnam,* 1972
- [ ] *The Conflict in Vietnam,* 1973
- [ ] *Customs and Culture of Vietnam,* 1966
- [ ] *Getting to Know the Vietnamese and Their Culture,* 1976
- [ ] *The History of the Vietnam War,* 1981
- [ ] *Let's Visit Vietnam,* 1966
- [ ] *Many Reasons Why: The American Involvement in Vietnam,* 1978
- [ ] *No More Vietnams? The War and the Future of American Foreign Policy,* 1968
- [ ] *Nobody Wanted War: Misperception in Vietnam and Other Wars,* 1968
- [ ] *On Strategy: A Critical Analysis of the Vietnam War,* 1982
- [ ] *Planning a Tragedy: The Americanization of the War in Vietnam,* 1982
- [ ] *P.O.W.: A Definitive History of the American Prisoner-of-War Experience in Vietnam, 1964–1973,* 1976
- [ ] *The President's War: The Story of the Tonkin Gulf Resolution and How the Nation Was Trapped in Vietnam,* 1971
- [ ] *The Real War: The Classic Reporting on the Vietnam War,* 1968
- [ ] *A Short History of the Vietnam War,* 1978
- [ ] *The Story of Vietnam: A Background Book for Young People,* 1966
- [ ] *Strategy for Defeat: Vietnam in Retrospect,* 1978
- [ ] *The Unfinished War: Vietnam and the American Conscience,* 1982
- [ ] *The United States in Vietnam: Misjudgment or Defense of Freedom?* 1975
- [ ] *Vietnam* [filmstrip], 1979
- [ ] *Vietnam Today: The Challenge of a Divided Nation,* 1966

960
Africa

GENERAL WEEDING
GUIDELINES

900s
5 to 15 years

Biography
5 to 10 years

Why Weed Africa?

Many school library media collections contain materials on Africa that are biased, dated, and inaccurate. This can result in students thinking of Africa as either a dry desert or a hot steaming jungle filled with wild animals and savage people, neither of which is a true image for this large and varied continent. Update your titles in this section to reflect Africa today.

Dewey Numbers to Check

Check the 960s (History of Africa) with specific emphasis on individual countries from 961 (Tunisia and Libya) to 968 (Republic of South Africa). Also check the travel and geography titles from 916.1 to 916.8 for all these respective areas. Review the reference and AV collections as well as the biography section.

Specific Criteria for Weeding

Check the bias of materials in your collection by reviewing both the text and the illustrations of titles. Africa is a huge land area with many diverse vegetation zones and ethnic groups. Be particularly aware of materials that refer to these ethnic groups as tribes, because Africans are culturally unified by their language, as are ethnic groups in Europe and other world regions. The term *tribe* implies a primitive and uncivilized people. Look for other terms that are viewed as outmoded or pejorative, such as *Bantu*, *Bushmen*, *Dark Continent*, *Hottentot*, *huts*, *primitive*, *Pygmies*, and *witch doctor*. Suggested topical activities for students should not reinforce negative stereotypes, such as shield-making projects. Keep a current atlas handy to check that countries represented by your collection still exist.

Tips for Replacing Titles

The political geography of Africa has changed many times in recent decades. Update maps and atlases as well as your travel and geography titles to reflect these changes. Be prepared to continually monitor the area and make changes as needed.

Consider Weeding Titles Like These

- [ ] *Africa Is People: Firsthand Accounts from Contemporary Africa*, 1967
- [ ] *Africa South of the Sahara*, 1962
- [ ] *The African Past: Chronicles from Antiquity to Modern Times*, 1964
- [ ] *Apartheid: A Documentary Study of Modern South Africa*, 1968
- [ ] *The Atlas of Africa*, 1973
- [ ] *Black Africa: Its Peoples and Their Cultures Today*, 1970
- [ ] *Camera on Africa: The World of an Ethiopian Boy*, 1970
- [ ] *Common Sense about Africa*, 1960
- [ ] *Contemporary Africa: Continent in Transition*, 1964
- [ ] *Discovering Black Africa* [filmstrip], 1970
- [ ] *Emerging African Nations and Their Leaders*, 1964
- [ ] *Ethiopia: A New Political History*, 1965
- [ ] *From Bush to City: A Look at the New Africa*, 1966
- [ ] *The Geography of Modern Africa*, 1964
- [ ] *The Land and People of Tanganyika*, 1963
- [ ] *Let's Visit Middle Africa: East Africa, Central Africa, the Congo*, 1958
- [ ] *Modern Libya: A Study in Political Development*, 1963
- [ ] *Ms. Africa: Profiles of Modern African Women*, 1973
- [ ] *The New Africans: A Guide to the Contemporary History of Emergent Africa and Its Leaders*, 1967
- [ ] *Rhodesia*, 1974
- [ ] *Teaching Africa Today: A Handbook for Teachers and Curriculum Planners*, 1973
- [ ] *Tropical Africa Today*, 1966
- [ ] *Understanding Egypt*, 1965
- [ ] *Women of Tropical Africa*, 1960

GENERAL WEEDING GUIDELINES

300s
5 to 20 years

900s
5 to 15 years

Biography
5 to 10 years

970.004
Native Americans

Why Weed Native Americans?

Several state K–12 educational standards require students to demonstrate that they are multiculturally sensitive citizens. Many stereotypes exist in literature, in movies and on television, in our minds, and in the minds of the young people we work with—especially when it comes to Native Americans. Working to rid your library media collection of old Native American stereotypes is a positive step for all.

Dewey Numbers to Check

Start by reviewing 970.004 (North American Native Peoples), the preferred classification for this topic. You should also check the optional classification of 970.1 (North American Native Peoples—Indians of North America). Other optional classification numbers are 970.3 (Specific Native Peoples) and 970.4 (Native Peoples in Specific Places in North America). While weeding the topic, you might consider making some decisions on reclassifying current titles and establishing a policy for future titles, remembering that 970.004 is now preferred. Check the 305.897s (Ethnic and National Groups—North American Native Peoples) for works that deal more with social issues than with history. Also check the reference, AV, fiction, and biography sections.

Specific Criteria for Weeding

Although date of publication is not always a clear indicator in weeding this or any other area, the publication in 1971 of *Bury My Heart at Wounded Knee* forever changed our perception of Native Americans. Anything published before that date should be examined carefully; however, stereotypes exist in materials published even today. Eliminate titles depicting Native Americans (by text or illustrations) as savages or as one people sharing common traits. Remember that there are many different native cultures, each with a unique language, dress, culture, and tradition. Most importantly, discard anything that you feel would embarrass or hurt a Native American child.

Tips for Replacing Titles

Stocking interesting biographies that are balanced and not judgmental can be the best way to counter stereotypes. Watch for favorably reviewed biographies on historical Native American figures such as Maria Tallchief, Jim Thorpe, Sitting Bull, Geronimo, Sequoyah, Sacajawea, Crazy Horse, Chief Joseph, Black Hawk, and Osceola.

Consider Weeding Titles Like These

- [ ] *10 Little Indians: The Counting Song and a Counting Book* [sound recording], 1977
- [ ] *The Amazing Red Man*, 1960
- [ ] *The American Indian: From Colonial Times to the Present*, 1974
- [ ] *The American Indian Then and Now*, 1957
- [ ] *American Indians: Yesterday and Today*, 1960
- [ ] *The Brave Little Indian*, 1951
- [ ] *The Complete Book of Indian Crafts and Lore*, 1954
- [ ] *Contemporary American Indian Leaders*, 1972
- [ ] *Crazy Horse: The Strange Man of the Oglalas*, 1942
- [ ] *David, Young Chief of the Quileutes: An American Indian Today*, 1967
- [ ] *First Book of Cowboys, Indians and Eskimos*, 1950
- [ ] *Heap Hungry Indian*, 1966
- [ ] *The How and Why Wonder Book of North American Indians*, 1965
- [ ] *How Medicine Man Cured Paleface Woman*, 1956
- [ ] *Indians at Home*, 1964
- [ ] *Indians, Indians, Indians: Stories of Tepees and Tomahawks, Wampum Belts and War Bonnets, Peace Pipes and Papooses*, 1950
- [ ] *Indians of the Southwest* [filmstrip], 1953
- [ ] *Indians on the Warpath*, 1957
- [ ] *Navaho Land: Yesterday and Today*, 1961
- [ ] *Our American Indians at a Glance*, 1961
- [ ] *Our Wild Indians: Thirty-three Years of Personal Experience among the Red Men of the Great West*, 1960
- [ ] *Red Children in White America*, 1977
- [ ] *Some People Are Indians*, 1974
- [ ] *The Tomahawk Family*, 1960
- [ ] *Two Little Savages: Being the Adventures of Two Boys Who Lived as Indians and What They Learned*, 1970

971–972
Canada and Mexico

Why Weed Canada and Mexico?

The United States is fortunate to have good neighbors: Canada and Mexico. But current events and security concerns demand that we look closer at our national borders and points of entry. With a Canadan/U.S. border of 4,121 miles and a Mexican/U.S. border of 2,062 miles, it is essential that we know our neighbors and provide up-to-date information for our students.

Dewey Numbers to Check

For history titles on both these countries, check 971 (Canada) and 972 (Mexico). The description and travel titles will be in 917.1 (Canada) and 917.2 (Mexico). Review the reference and the AV collections also.

Specific Criteria for Weeding

Many of the K–12 titles (both print and AV) published about these countries from the 1960s through the 1980s have a simplistic view of Canada and Mexico. This can be confusing and misleading to students hearing current discussions on the national news regarding security issues, visa restrictions, immigration, and border patrols. It also does a disservice to both countries to not acknowledge their diversities and current conditions. Pay special attention to the national news regarding Canada and Mexico for a month and then look at your collection. See the difference? Weed any titles that seem superficial, patronizing, or inaccurate.

Tips for Replacing Titles

The publishing market tends to follow demand, so the relatively low K–12 demand for this topic means limited replacement titles are available for Mexico and especially Canada. That's no excuse to keep outdated titles when there are many other sources of current information such as the Internet. Weed your outdated titles, know your print and AV collections, and be prepared to fill those collection gaps as new titles are released.

Consider Weeding Titles Like These

☐ *Activities and Projects: Mexico in Color,* 1977

☐ *The Architecture of Mexico: Yesterday and Today,* 1969

☐ *A Book to Begin on the Indians of Mexico,* 1967

☐ *Canada: A Modern History,* 1960

☐ *Canada: A Regional Study* [filmstrip], 1972

☐ *Canada and the USA: A Background Book about Internal Conflict and the New Nationalism,* 1972

☐ *Canada: Challenge of Change* [filmstrip], 1977

☐ *Canada: The Land and Its People,* 1976

☐ *Crafts of Mexico,* 1977

☐ *Exploring Canada from Sea to Sea,* 1967

☐ *The Friendly Frontier: The Story of the Canadian-American Border,* 1962

☐ *Getting to Know Mexico,* 1959

☐ *Guide to All Mexico,* 1973

☐ *A History of Mexico: From Pre-Columbia to Present,* 1978

☐ *How People Live in Canada,* 1971

☐ *How People Live in Mexico,* 1969

☐ *The Land and People of Canada,* 1960

☐ *The Land and People of Mexico,* 1964

☐ *Living in Mexico Today* [filmstrip], 1967

☐ *Mexico: Facing Tomorrow's Challenges* [filmstrip], 1977

☐ *Mexico Today,* 1972

☐ *Our Neighbor, Mexico* [filmstrip], 1975

☐ *The Real Book about Canada,* 1959

☐ *This Is Canada: History and Growth,* 1965

☐ *The United States and Canada: Present and Future,* 1978

972.91
Cuba

Why Weed Cuba?

Cuba has been in the news often in the past several years, from the Elian Gonzalez situation in Miami (1999–2000) to the continuing speculation on future leadership of Cuba because of the age of its long-time ruler/president Fidel Castro (1926–). Aside from the political news, there is also a new infatuation with Cuban/Latino music and culture here in the United States, and travel buffs are eagerly awaiting the anticipated opening of travel to Cuba. School library media collections on Cuba should be current enough to support this interest.

Dewey Numbers to Check

Check 972.91 (Cuba) for the history of that country. Also review 917.291 for Cuban geography and travel titles. Because of the long and contentious diplomatic relations between the United States and Cuba after the 1959 takeover by Castro, check the 327s (International Relations), 973.92 (U.S. History 1953–2001), and 973.93 (U.S. History 2001–) for titles including U.S./Cuban incidents and issues. Check the reference and AV collections as well as the biographies for the few (but important) personalities there.

Specific Criteria for Weeding

Cuban history titles published since 1959 should be carefully reviewed to see if any speculations and interpretations included are still valid. As with all history titles, primary source materials are acceptable, but perhaps not analysis of years past or dated projections for the future. The continued trade embargoes and the illicit migration of Cuban citizens to the United States should be presented in a current as well as historical framework. Although time may seem to stand still in a country that still drives and maintains American cars from the 1950s, there is no reason to keep dated travel and description titles—in print or AV format.

Tips for Replacing Titles

Check the age of your biography of Fidel Castro. Although the last chapter has still not been written, any biography of him should be fairly recent. Be prepared to replace even those recent biography titles once this aging Communist leader of Cuba for over forty years is gone.

Consider Weeding Titles Like These

- 90 Miles from Home: The Face of Cuba Today, 1961
- Background to Revolution: The Development of Modern Cuba, 1979
- Castro, the Kremlin, and Communism in Latin America, 1969
- Castro's Cuba: An American Dilemma, 1962
- Castro's Revolution: Myths and Realities, 1962
- The Complete Travel Guide to Cuba, 1979
- Cuba and the United States: Long Range Perspectives, 1967
- Cuba, Castro, and the United States, 1971
- Cuba: Continuing Crisis, 1979
- Cuba for Beginners: An Illustrated Guide for Americans (and Their Government), 1970
- Cuba in Pictures, 1974
- Cuba: Its People, Its Society, Its Culture, 1962
- Cuba: The Island Country [filmstrip], 1973
- Cuba Under Castro [motion picture], 1966
- Cubans in Exile: Disaffection and the Revolution, 1968
- Cubans in the United States [filmstrip], 1981
- Fidel: A Biography of Fidel Castro, 1986
- Fidel Castro: Rebel-Liberator or Dictator? 1959
- Getting to Know Cuba, 1962
- Inside Cuba Today, 1978
- The Land and People of Cuba, 1973
- Let's Visit Cuba, 1983
- The New Cuba: Paradoxes and Potentials, 1976
- No Free Lunch: Food and Revolution in Cuba Today, 1984
- What Happened in Cuba? A Documentary History, 1963

973
U.S. Presidents

GENERAL WEEDING GUIDELINES

300s
5 to 20 years

900s
5 to 15 years

Biography
5 to 10 years

Why Weed U.S. Presidents?

Many students are most familiar with only three U.S. presidents: Washington, Lincoln, and the current president. The K–12 library media collection should help fill in those gaps. Make sure you have titles that cover the presidents up to the present administration and that do not stop with Johnson (1963–1969), Nixon (1969–1974), Ford (1974–1977), Carter (1977–1981), Reagan (1981–1989), G. H. W. Bush (1989–1993), or Clinton (1993–2001). Weed the outdated titles and replace with some of the many new titles on the market today.

Dewey Numbers to Check

Review the history of the presidents and their administrations in the 973s (United States). Check the 321.8s (Democratic Government) for general information on this government type. Next check the 352.23s (Chief Executives) for more information on this specific position, and check for any titles in the former number of 321—if you have any, weed them or move them to the current classification of 352.23. Check the biography section, both collective and individual. Finally, check the reference and AV collections.

Specific Criteria for Weeding

Any title that implies it is a review of all presidents (or first ladies) should be up to date with the current presidency. Don't keep anything of this nature on the shelf if it is older than five years. Titles on individual presidents can be older if still considered accurate and impartial. Remember that history can and does change the perception of presidents and their administrations. Be especially wary of titles published during a president's term of office—it is better to have the perspective from the completed term.

Tips for Replacing Titles

You may want to build your collection in this topic on specific presidents according to your local demand or the publication market. As an example, there are many excellent new titles on Lincoln available today.

Consider Weeding Titles Like These

- [ ] *1600 Pennsylvania Avenue: Presidents and the People since 1929*, 1963
- [ ] *The American Heritage Pictorial History of the Presidents of the United States*, 1968
- [ ] *American Presidents and the Presidency*, 1972
- [ ] *America's First Ladies 1865–Present Day*, 1968
- [ ] *The Biggest Job in the World: The American Presidency*, 1964
- [ ] *A Book to Begin on the White House*, 1962
- [ ] *The Contemporary Presidency*, 1976
- [ ] *Facts about the Presidents*, 1959
- [ ] *Famous American Presidents* [filmstrip], 1978
- [ ] *The First Book of Presidents*, 1961
- [ ] *The First Book of Vice-Presidents of the United States*, 1977
- [ ] *First Ladies*, 1962
- [ ] *The Future of the American Presidency*, 1975
- [ ] *Hail to the Chief! The Inauguration Days of Our Presidents*, 1965

- [ ] *A History of the Presidential Elections*, 1964
- [ ] *The Look-It-Up Book of Presidents*, 1968
- [ ] *The Mass Media Election: How Americans Choose Their President*, 1980
- [ ] *Our Seven Greatest Presidents*, 1964
- [ ] *Pictorial History of American Presidents*, 1964
- [ ] *The Power of the Modern Presidency*, 1974
- [ ] *The Presidency Today*, 1956
- [ ] *Scandals in the Highest Office: Facts and Fictions in the Private Lives of Our Presidents*, 1973
- [ ] *The Second Man: The Changing Role of the Vice Presidency*, 1968
- [ ] *The White House: A History of the Presidents*, 1972
- [ ] *The White House and Its Thirty-two Families*, 1965

973.7
The Civil War

Why Weed the Civil War?

When it comes to the Civil War, you can count on two things in any school library media center: Teachers will assign reports on the topic, and publishers will continue to supply the market with a steady stream of new titles each year on this high-interest subject. You probably have a relatively large selection of titles on the Civil War, many of them well worn from years of use for reports. The trick is to weed the old and update with new titles without disruption to the students and teachers.

Dewey Numbers to Check

Check the 973.7s (Administration of Abraham Lincoln, 1861–1865—Civil War) for most titles. Then check the biography (both collective and individual) as well as the fiction sections. Finally, check the reference and AV collections.

Specific Criteria for Weeding

Time the weeding of this section carefully so you are not caught short of titles when report time rolls around. Adding replacement titles before weeding the old ones might be wise. Check with teachers before discarding old print titles (but not old filmstrips—dump them!) to be sure you are not jeopardizing classroom assignments. Never weed primary source materials or any local or state history titles of that era unless a replacement has been obtained. Question any older nonfiction title that implies it is a current-day reassessment or a complete account because assessments change over time and new information continually becomes available in this popular topic.

Tips for Replacing Titles

Be careful when purchasing nonfiction titles from one of the popular series publications. Although one or two titles in the series may receive a positive review, the rest might not be up to the same standard. Check for individual reviews. Purchase new, attractive editions of well-known fiction classics to increase their appeal to your readers and add some of the newer nonseries titles on the market today.

Consider Weeding Titles Like These

- [ ] *Across Five Aprils* [filmstrip], 1974
- [ ] *America Divided: The Civil War and Reconstruction* [filmstrip], 1984
- [ ] *Americans Interpret Their Civil War*, 1962
- [ ] *Best Photos of the Civil War*, 1961
- [ ] *Books Relating to the Civil War: A Priced Check List, Including Regimental Histories, Lincolniana and Confederate Imprints*, 1962
- [ ] *Causes of the Civil War: Institutional Failure or Human Blunder?* 1982
- [ ] *The Civil War: A Complete Military History*, 1981
- [ ] *The Civil War: An Unvarnished Account of the Late but Still Lively Hostilities*, 1953
- [ ] *Civil War and Reconstruction* [filmstrip], 1970
- [ ] *Civil War Collector's Encyclopedia: Arms, Uniforms, and Equipment of the Union and Confederacy*, 1963
- [ ] *The Civil War: Its Background and Causes* [filmstrip], 1982
- [ ] *The Civil War: Strange and Fascinating Facts*, 1960
- [ ] *The Civil War through the Camera: A Complete Illustrated History of the Civil War*, 1979

- [ ] *A Concise Encyclopedia of the Civil War*, 1965
- [ ] *The Golden Book of the Civil War*, 1974
- [ ] *The Legacy of the Civil War*, 1964
- [ ] *Lincoln and the Civil War* [filmstrip], 1975
- [ ] *Lincoln Reconsidered: Essays on the Civil War Era*, 1956
- [ ] *The Negro in the Civil War*, 1953
- [ ] *The Photographic History of the Civil War*, 1957
- [ ] *Rifles for Watie* [filmstrip], 1972
- [ ] *Since the Civil War*, 1926
- [ ] *The Social Fabric: American Life from the Civil War to the Present*, 1975
- [ ] *Stonewall Jackson and the American Civil War: A Modern Abridgment*, 1968
- [ ] *Voices of Blue and Gray: The Civil War* [filmstrip], 1973

GENERAL WEEDING GUIDELINES

This new topic should be weeded earlier than standard guidelines indicate.

973.93
September 11

Why Weed September 11?

To provide information about September 11, 2001, for your students, you may have purchased some materials that were rushed to publication to fill the nationwide demand. Some of those titles were great, and some were not. Some of the titles may now be worn out by that initial demand and are due for replacement. Now is a good time to review this section. Weed, replace, and add so you have a solid collection on this topic of continuing interest.

Dewey Numbers to Check

Look in the 973.93s (United States 2001–) for titles on this topic classed according to the period of the attacks. Also look at the 974.7s (New York), 974.8s (Pennsylvania), and 975.3s (District of Columbia) for titles that approach the subject according to the attack area. Although the reference section may not have titles on this subject, the AV collection probably does and should be checked.

Specific Criteria for Weeding

The weeding criteria for this section include evaluating titles according to content, tone, and sensitivity. Examine the content of the titles by looking for signs of information padding, poor or repeated photos within the same work, and careless editing. Be especially aware that some series created for the topic were rushed to publication, and some of the titles within such series have not received positive reviews. As for tone and sensitivity, though the national emotion and impact of the events of that day should be honestly represented, be careful not to keep titles that play on that emotion with an overly dramatic or fatalistic approach. Students need information, not a sense of panic, fear, or helplessness. The photos and text should also clearly represent the facts of the event, but not unduly contribute to negative stereotyping of ethnic or religious groups as a whole.

Tips for Replacing Titles

Because September 11 redefined terrorism for this country, some recent titles on that topic in your collection may be dated. Check the content to determine whether it includes September 11 by looking for that event even if the publication date was 2001.

Consider Weeding Titles Like These

- [ ] *9.11.01: Terrorists Attack the U.S.*, 2002
- [ ] *America Under Attack: September 11, 2001*, 2001
- [ ] *Attack on America: The Day the Twin Towers Collapsed*, 2002
- [ ] *The Attacks on the World Trade Center, February 26, 1993, and September 11, 2001*, 2002
- [ ] *Helping Hands: A City and a Nation Lend Their Support at Ground Zero*, 2002
- [ ] *September 11, 2001: A Simple Account for Children*, 2002
- [ ] *Terrorism*, 2002
- [ ] *Terrorism: A World of Shadows* [videorecording], 2001
- [ ] *Terrorism in America*, 2003

[*Note*: Because of the recency of this event and because publications have only been available since 2001, our list of titles to consider weeding is short.]

Fic
Fiction

GENERAL WEEDING
GUIDELINES

Fiction
5 to 15 years

Why Weed Fiction?

The fiction section in most school library media centers contains two main types of titles: classics/award winners and popular interest. Those classic and award-winning titles are easily weeded based on the condition of the title and the physical appeal of the format. Weeding the popular interest titles is more complicated because most should reflect the interests of the current student population and not those of earlier generations.

Dewey Numbers to Check

Most fiction titles in K–12 collections are grouped in one physical location, usually labeled *fiction*. However, you may have some specialty collections such as mysteries, science fiction, and graphic novels. Some titles (mainly classic works) may be shelved in the 800s according to the language of the work.

Specific Criteria for Weeding

Look at the classic/award-winning titles and be sure they are attractive new editions. If not, replace them. Historical fiction often bridges the classic and popular interest categories. Be sure these titles are still historically accurate and are not biased toward any group.

Weeding popular interest fiction titles requires a ruthless approach. If a title has not circulated in the past two or three years, you can probably discard it. In addition to circulation, look for stereotyping or gender, racial, or religious bias. Consider whether a student would be misled or feel diminished by reading the title. Also carefully check popular interest reading titles that focus on vocational or career themes to be sure the information is still valid.

Tips for Replacing Titles

Fiction titles, especially those classed as popular interest, often are means for students to develop life skills and social attitudes, so it is important to keep them timely. Rely on reviews for help in selection, and then track the circulation of new purchases to determine what is really popular with the students in your school.

Consider Weeding Titles Like These

- [ ] *The African Witch*, 1936
- [ ] *Akavak: An Eskimo Journey*, 1968
- [ ] *The Blacker the Berry: A Novel of Negro Life*, 1972
- [ ] *The Bobbsey Twins Camping Out*, 1923
- [ ] *The Brave Little Indian*, 1951
- [ ] *Bud Plays Junior High Football*, 1957
- [ ] *The Busiest Boy in Holland*, 1959
- [ ] *Candy Stripers*, 1958
- [ ] *A Cap for Mary Ellis*, 1953
- [ ] *Carol Goes Backstage*, 1941
- [ ] *Cherry Ames, Army Nurse*, 1944
- [ ] *Chi-Wee: The Adventures of a Little Indian Girl*, 1925
- [ ] *Clarence the TV Dog*, 1955
- [ ] *Copy Girl*, 1959
- [ ] *Country Fireman*, 1948
- [ ] *The Cub Scout Mystery*, 1952
- [ ] *Dan Frontier Goes Hunting*, 1962
- [ ] *Date with a Career*, 1958
- [ ] *Fireman for a Day*, 1952
- [ ] *First Boy on the Moon*, 1959
- [ ] *Freddy and the Men from Mars*, 1954
- [ ] *Girls Can Dream, Too!* 1948
- [ ] *The Green Man from Space*, 1955
- [ ] *Mommies at Work*, 1961
- [ ] *The Soul Brothers and Sister Lou*, 1968

REF
Reference

Why Weed Reference?

As virtual reference services continue to grow in both numbers and popularity, print reference collections cannot stay static or bloated if they are going to be viable and useful in a K–12 library media collection. Even more than the rest of your collection, titles in reference must be current and authoritative.

Dewey Numbers to Check

Your reference section may be small, but the Dewey range is large! Your reference collection probably spans all the Dewey classes. And if you have a ready-reference section behind your desk, you'll need to check it also.

Specific Criteria for Weeding

As you examine each title in your reference collection, you will need to decide whether to keep it as reference, move it to circulation, or discard it. A title kept as reference must be up to date as well as formatted for efficient reference use. Any titles more suited for browsing but still current should be moved to circulation. Items with *encyclopedia* or *dictionary* in their titles should not automatically merit a place in your reference collection. Evaluate all items. Be critical in all areas, but especially in technical, political, or medical topics. Even titles on subject areas like cookery and social behavior can have misleading or potentially dangerous information for today's students.

Reference titles are often updated by new editions or supplements. If a new edition has been issued, you should replace your older version. Be sure that you keep up with any supplements until a new edition is released. (But be careful that you don't mistakenly discard the latest edition and keep only the supplement!)

Tips for Replacing Titles

Update your old standards, but also think in terms of new topics that students might look for in a print reference resource as well as online. Watch as new reference titles are published and decide if the topic would be in demand for your reference section. When your new purchases arrive, promote both the new titles and your print reference section.

Consider Weeding Titles Like These

☐ *The Aerospace Age Dictionary*, 1965

☐ *American Indians, Yesterday and Today: A Profusely Illustrated Encyclopedia of the American Indian*, 1960

☐ *The Ann Landers Encyclopedia, A to Z: Improve Your Life Emotionally, Medically, Sexually, Socially, Spiritually*, 1978

☐ *The Baseball Encyclopedia: The Complete and Official Record of Major League Baseball*, 1969

☐ *Better Homes and Gardens Encyclopedia of Cooking*, 1973

☐ *Black's Medical Dictionary*, 1976

☐ *Clements' Encyclopedia of World Governments*, 1974

☐ *Computer Dictionary for Everyone*, 1979

☐ *The Condensed Chemical Dictionary*, 1971

☐ *A Consumer's Dictionary of Food Additives*, 1972

☐ *Geography: A Reference Handbook*, 1968

☐ *Hammond Advanced Reference Atlas: A Complete Social Studies Atlas in Four Parts Showing the Geographical Setting of the Modern, Medieval and Ancient World*, 1968

☐ *Handbook of Chemistry and Physics: A Ready-Reference Book of Chemical and Physical Data*, 1966

☐ *Harper Encyclopedia of the Modern World: A Concise Reference History from 1760 to the Present*, 1970

☐ *Henley's Formulas for Home and Workshop: Containing Ten Thousand Selected Household, Workshop, and Scientific Formulas, Trade Secrets, Food and Chemical Recipes, Processes, and Money Saving Ideas; A Valuable Reference Book for the Home, the Factory, the Office, and the Workshop*, 1979

☐ *How to Do Library Research*, 1975

☐ *Index to Women of the World from Ancient to Modern Times: Biographies and Portraits*, 1970

☐ *Instant Medical Adviser*, 1980

☐ *Know About Horses: A Ready Reference Guide to Horses, Horse People, and Horse Sports*, 1961

☐ *Disabilities: A Reference Book*, 1980

☐ *McGraw-Hill Encyclopedia of Science and Technology: An International Reference Work in Fifteen Volumes Including an Index*, 1977

☐ *The New York Times Guide to Reference Materials*, 1971

☐ *North American Reference Encyclopedia of Ecology and Pollution*, 1972

☐ *Quick Reference Encyclopedia: The Complete Reference Handbook of Basic Knowledge for Home, School, and Office*, 1976

☐ *Religions in America: A Completely Revised and Up-to-Date Guide to Churches and Religious Groups in the United States*, 1963

SC
Short Stories

GENERAL WEEDING GUIDELINES

800s
5 to 15 years

SC
5 to 15 years

Why Weed Short Stories?

How popular are the short stories in your collection? If the section is used only when required for classroom assignments, try weeding out-of-date titles and adding some new high-interest titles. This might tempt some students to browse and read this wonderful genre without that assignment in hand.

Dewey Numbers to Check

In many K–12 library media collections, the short stories are shelved in a separate location, sometimes labeled SC for "story collection." However, you may have some scattered in the 800s (Literature) according to the language of the collection. Check the reference and the AV sections also.

Specific Criteria for Weeding

Always remember that any indexed collection of short stories has immunity from weeding unless it is in terrible physical condition! Never incur the wrath of the English teachers by discarding a source unless all stories are available in other collections. If in doubt, check with your teachers before discarding a title. However, old filmstrips should not be maintained in a current library AV collection. If one of your teachers still insists on using them, remove them from your collection and give them to the teacher.

Concentrate your short story weeding efforts on those collections aimed at leisure reading by students. Anything on the topics of hobbies, humor, special interests, dating, growing up, or school life should be carefully reviewed to see if it is of any interest to today's students. If the item was published as little as ten years ago, it probably is too old to be of current interest.

Tips for Replacing Titles

With an aim of increasing global awareness and supporting the diversity of your students, purchase more short story collections with a national or an ethnic focus. After reviewing your current short story titles for inaccuracy, misleading information, bias, or insensitive portrayals, replace offenders with new titles that are both balanced and attractive.

Consider Weeding Titles Like These

- [ ] *Action Stories of Yesterday and Today,* 1971
- [ ] *African Short Stories: A Collection of Contemporary African Writing,* 1970
- [ ] *All Kinds of Courage: Stories about Boys and Girls of Yesterday and Today,* 1962
- [ ] *American Short Stories: 1820 to the Present,* 1964
- [ ] *American Short Stories since 1945,* 1968
- [ ] *The Boys' Life Book of Baseball Stories,* 1964
- [ ] *Brothers and Sisters: Modern Stories by Black Americans,* 1970
- [ ] *Contemporary Chinese Stories,* 1968
- [ ] *Contemporary Latin American Short Stories,* 1974
- [ ] *Every Boy's Book of Outer Space Stories,* 1960
- [ ] *Feminine Plural: Stories by Women about Growing Up,* 1972
- [ ] *Getting the Most Out of Life: An Anthology from the Reader's Digest,* 1946
- [ ] *Girls, Girls, Girls: Stories of Love, Courage and the Quest for Happiness,* 1957
- [ ] *In Bikole: Eight Modern Stories about Life in a West African Village,* 1978
- [ ] *In the Looking Glass: Twenty-one Modern Short Stories by Women,* 1977
- [ ] *Introduction to American Short Stories* [film-strip], 1976
- [ ] *Julie Eisenhower's Favorite Stories,* 1974
- [ ] *Love Comes Riding: Stories of Romance and Adventure for Girls,* 1929
- [ ] *Modern Arabic Short Stories,* 1967
- [ ] *New Voices: Contemporary Soviet Short Stories,* 1966
- [ ] *The Other Side of Tomorrow: Original Science Fiction Stories about Young People of the Future,* 1973
- [ ] *Stories Boys Like,* 1965
- [ ] *Stories of School and College Life: September to June,* 1942
- [ ] *Stories of the Modern South,* 1978
- [ ] *Teenage Humorous Stories,* 1957

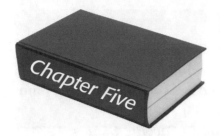

What Automation Hath Wrought

USING YOUR ONLINE CATALOG AND CIRCULATION SYSTEM IN WEEDING

Most schools have automated circulation and catalog systems. These can be very useful in the weeding process, allowing you to do some things that were not easily accomplished before this technology was available. Although there are a variety of automation systems and each has its own unique features, your system may be able to help you identify titles that need to be reevaluated.

Your circulation system may allow you to print circulation reports within a specific period—the last year, the last five years, and so on. (You'll need to have had the system long enough to have accumulated some history for the collection.) Print a report and then look at the items that have circulated the most. Are they in need of repair? Should they be replaced? Are there newer editions available? Now look at items that haven't circulated at all in the last few years. Are they still relevant to the curriculum? To your students? Are they up to date? Accurate? Visually appealing? Would they circulate if you promoted them to teachers and students? Should they circulate more, or is there a good reason that they haven't?

Online Public Access Catalogs (OPACs) can be useful, too. Again, each may have differing capabilities. If yours allows you to search by date, choose a subject and search for materials in the collection published before 1950. If you find few or no items, good for you! Now search the same subject for materials published between 1950 and 1960, then 1960 to

1970, and so on. How ruthless and rigorous you want to be will depend upon the size of your collection, the importance of that subject to students and teachers, and other resources available on the topic.

Remember, just because materials are old doesn't mean they must be discarded. They may be classics, contain good photographs or unusual illustrations, or contain local information not widely available. They may provide needed balance for a topic or they may be rare, valuable titles. Your OPAC will simply help you identify titles at which you might want to take a closer look.

Another good trick for using your OPAC in weeding is to identify titles that may contain words that imply they are current, and then to examine the date of publication or the copyright date. Many systems will allow you to do both at the same time.

Search for titles that include these words: *now, today, modern, contemporary, nowadays, recent, current, new, present, present-day, prevalent,* or *prevailing.* Limit by date if you can. Look at the date of publication for each title found. *Afghanistan Today,* published in 1979, is very different from *Afghanistan Today* with a publication date of 1999. Reexamine any materials that may be sending the wrong message or conveying inaccurate information. Discard them if they are. Also look at the physical condition and circulation records of older materials.

COMMERCIAL COLLECTION DEVELOPMENT AND ANALYSIS SERVICES

Another advantage of library automation for school library media centers is that many catalog and circulation system vendors are now offering collection analysis and development services, and most of them are free. Because your records are in standard electronic format (MARC), this is easy to do. The accuracy of the analysis, of course, depends upon the data you provide being complete and accurate.

You may be asked to export your data in a particular format and send it to the company on CD-ROM. Some vendors provide a way to upload your collection data online right from your office or from home. These services help identify strengths and weaknesses of your collection by comparing it to those of other schools, to award-winning collections, or to "average" collections. Reports generally include impressive and easy to understand charts and graphs, and these are useful in communicating collection needs and strengths to parents, teachers, and administrators.

Why are these services free? Most companies hope, of course, that when you purchase new titles, you will order from them, but this is not required. Check with your own automation company to see what services it offers and what costs might be applied.

If you do use a commercial collection analysis service, be sure you understand what criteria are being applied and what comparisons are being made. Some companies recommend that items be no older than twenty years, while others may recommend ten or twelve. Some compare your collection to those of award-winning schools while others may compare to a district average or to schools that are strong in areas different from those your curriculum emphasizes.

Some services will print a list of your entire collection for you in Dewey order along with new titles recommended for purchase based on authoritative recommendation, popularity, or both. That way you can see not only what you have and what might be tossed but what is available to replace your weeded works.

FUTURE DEVELOPMENTS

Technology is advancing rapidly in many areas, and technology for school library media centers is changing as well, although because of funding, perhaps not as rapidly as we would like. Academic, public, special, and some school librarians are beginning to explore new technologies that may track both objective data (such as publication date, length of time in the collection, and use) and subjective data (such as keyword analysis in relation to the curriculum or contemporary practice). Current technologies such as radio frequency identification (RFID) tags are being tested and used in large public and academic libraries in the United States and elsewhere. Although there is some controversy regarding privacy issues when using RFID tags for individuals' library cards, the technology is quite established in businesses for inventory control.

RFID tags may soon replace both barcodes and security labels. They have the capacity to access databases that hold much more information, such as circulation data, keywords or tags, bibliographic information, and more. One advantage of RFID is that you do not have to handle each item to read it because it uses a radio signal. A receiver with a small antenna can read the information without the item being scanned directly; in fact, it doesn't even have to be within the line of sight of the receiver! Should this technology become affordable and practical for K–12 schools, it would allow you to combine shelf reading, inventory, and weeding. It is possible that the items weeded could even be removed from the catalog data automatically!

The technology can also be used to track down lost or misplaced materials. For more information, search the Web for the current status of RFID and libraries. Also, see http://www.ala.org/ala/oif/ifissues/rfid.htm for a discussion of the potential positive and negative impacts of this technology.

Currently, Wal-Mart is requiring its top one hundred suppliers to use RFID tags on products sold to Wal-Mart, and the company will use them first for inventory control in its warehouses. RFID can also be used to track inventory on the shelves—telling managers how many boxes of a product are on the shelf and indicating when to reorder based on data about how fast the product sells. Testing is under way in several stores, and, when the technology is fully implemented, checkout may be a matter of rolling your cart through the checkout, not passing each item through a scanner. The same RFID code may one day be read by your refrigerator, telling you how old your orange juice is and when it was last used! Even non-techie librarians can begin to see some interesting possibilities for RFID in their own settings: inventory, self-checkout, locating lost or misshelved materials, circulation data, and more!

Similarly, Digital Library Assistants (DLAs), powerful handheld computers, are getting a great deal of interest. Information can be loaded onto a DLA from the computer or via a small flash memory card. The information available to the DLA may include copyright or publication date and information about circulation. That data could help in making decisions about items to be weeded.

Library automation companies are partnering with a wide variety of companies that provide technology solutions in other settings, and it is likely that systems will continue to make school library media specialists more productive, providing more time for you to work with teachers and students. Watch for news about these developments in professional publications and ask about them at conferences.

Once you've identified items to be removed from the collection, there are a few more things you must do. One is to decide what to do with those materials you no longer want on the shelves. You also need to clean up your records, removing the item from the shelflist (if you have one) and the catalog. Finally, you must consider adding new titles to the collection.

WHAT TO DO WITH ITEMS YOU'VE REMOVED FROM THE SHELVES

Most districts or schools with a weeding policy will specify what to do with items that have been weeded. If this is true for your library media center, be sure to follow that policy.

If you think about it, there are really only two choices: (1) keep it or (2) get rid of it! Although that sounds simple, it is a decision based on your professional judgment, your school library media program, your collection, and your school community. You must make the decision.

Keeping an Item

You may want to keep an item in your collection if the information is current and relevant, even though it has not circulated in a while or just doesn't look too appealing. Maybe a little promotion—displaying it, book-talking it, making it more visible—is what is needed. Perhaps students can bring new life to these items by creating new covers or packaging with the help of an art teacher!

On occasion, you may want to keep an item until the next weeding because it is in an area in which you do not have sufficient coverage, because it is curriculum-related now but the curriculum will be changing and the item may not be needed in the future, or because *most* of it is current and accurate, but a small portion is now out of date. In these cases, make a note that it should be discarded in the next weeding and why, and, to save time and effort, mark the item in some way to make clear it needs to go when that section is weeded again.

If an item is important to the collection, current, and used but in poor physical condition, you may want to mend it, clean it, or even rebind it. However, you might want to see if another copy or a newer edition is available and replace it. Repair is time-consuming and rebinding is expensive.

Getting Rid of an Item

Whatever you do, discard judiciously and in accordance with policy. Again, we favor weeding a little at a time so that you won't need to deal with massive piles of discards at any one time.

There are several ways to eliminate an item from your collection. You will need to consider each item and the best way to remove it. You may be instructed to ship unusable materials to the district office. In that case, it becomes someone else's problem. If your school or district does not have a discard policy, consider the following.

> *Donate it.* If the information is accurate and the item is in good condition but it is not appropriate for your students, donate it to another school where it will be used. You can also donate usable duplicate copies to classrooms, other school libraries, public libraries, schools, hospitals, or other organizations where the title might be used. You might want to circulate a list of what is available and let others select what they can use so that your weeded items don't become someone else's problems. Do not donate out-of-date, inaccurate, or unusable materials to anyone. If it isn't good enough for your students, it isn't good enough for teachers, "poor" school or public libraries, nursing homes, correctional facilities, or children in third world countries. Bad information is bad information.

> *Recycle it.* Books are made of paper, and a recycling facility may be able to use the pages. Check with your community recycling agencies. Some do accept books and some do not, but they will accept magazines, newspapers, vendor catalogs, paperbacks, and other formats.

> *Sell it.* Depending upon your school and district policies, you may be able to sell unwanted but usable materials to a used-book

dealer or even at your own used-materials sale and put the money you receive into new materials. Be sure to clear this with your administration, remove ownership labels, and mark each item *Discard* so it doesn't come back to you—in any way!

Discard it. You may have to destroy some items or just throw them in the trash. This sometimes upsets the school community—especially if they are not informed about the purpose for weeding or if large quantities of discarded items appear in the dumpster or local landfill. Make special arrangements or discard a few at a time. Although you may not have to explain why those in poor physical condition were discarded, you may have to justify those that were withdrawn for other reasons. Be prepared. Remember to keep a few good examples of "bad" titles to show parents, teachers, and administrators why weeding is critical.

Finally, make it a policy never to make weeded items your own. If it's good enough for you, it probably could be sold or donated. You won't want to look like you've weeded to build your own personal collection. That could even result in criminal charges!

UPDATING YOUR RECORDS

Keeping your catalog up to date is critical, whether it is a card catalog or an online catalog. If you have a separate automated circulation system, you'll want to remove records from it as well. If you maintain a shelflist, you must also keep it current. For each item you are removing from the collection:

Stamp the item *DISCARD* or *WEEDED*.

Remove or obliterate any ownership marks, book pockets, and/or barcodes.

Remove the item from the record database(s): card catalog, online catalog, circulation system, and/or shelflist.

Keep a record of what you have discarded and why. (If you're using an automated circulation system, you can create "patrons" called Discarded to Classroom, Discarded Obsolete, Discarded Worn, and so on, and check out the item to these patrons. At the end of the weeding period, print a report and delete the items from the system.)

Dispose of the item according to district policy or in one of the methods previously mentioned.

If your collection is part of a larger collection, such as a district, regional, or state union catalog, or part of a multitype cooperative, remember to report deletions to the larger catalog in whatever way has been designated for maintenance. Some union catalogs are "live" and the change will be recorded immediately. Others may ask for a shelflist card, a bibliographic entry, a file of MARC records, or other notation of deletion.

Annette Lamb and Larry Johnson, *Collection Maintenance and Weeding,* http://eduscapes.com/sms/weeding.html.

Never let your catalog—or your union catalog—get out of sync with the collection. Cleaning up a catalog is extremely painful and time-consuming.

ADDING TO THE COLLECTION

Not every item that is deleted from the collection needs to be replaced, but in areas where the collection lacks scope or depth, or for items that have been removed because they have been superseded by new editions or because they get a great deal of use and are in poor physical condition, replacement titles should be considered. In addition, as curriculum and students' interests change, you will want to add titles to supplement the collection in some areas.

Popular works will generally have newer editions with updated information, illustrations, and covers. For other titles, the weeding criteria for each topic in chapter 4 will also provide some hints about what to look for in newer titles. Additionally, we have provided some general tips under each topic.

The collection is central to any library media program. Although there is seldom enough money to have the kind of collection you dream about, there's a real danger that—unless weeded frequently and ruthlessly—your collection can become a nightmare. One of the joys of being a library media specialist is using your professional skills to enable students and teachers to locate, evaluate, and use information. Be sure your professionalism is obvious to everyone through the selection, retention, and weeding of library media materials so that your collection reflects the curriculum, current events, and students' needs and interests.

WEEDING RESOURCES
ON THE WORLD WIDE WEB

Alternative Basic Library Education. *Weeding the Collection.*
http://www.lili.org/forlibs/ce/able/course4/01index.htm.

> From the Idaho State Library, an online weeding course in five
> parts designed for library staff members who have no formal
> training.

American Library Association. 2004. *Weeding Library Collections: A
Selected Annotated Bibliography for Library Collection Evaluation* (ALA
Library Fact Sheet #15). http://www.ala.org/Template.cfm?Section
=libraryfactsheet&Template=/ContentManagement/ContentDisplay.cfm&
ContentID=75744 *or* http://tinyurl.com/4y8qc.

> This annotated bibliography specifically addresses weeding.

Arizona State Library. *Weeding.* http://www.lib.az.us/cdt/weeding.htm.

> Part of a comprehensive site designed for small and rural libraries.
> Provides a good overview of weeding.

Bertland, L. *Resources for School Librarians—Collection Development:
Evaluation and Weeding.* http://www.sldirectory.com/libsf/resf/coldev2
.html#weed.

> Links to tools and articles about assessment and weeding.

Boon, B. 1995. *The CREW Method: Expanded Guidelines for Collection
Evaluation and Weeding for Small and Medium-Sized Public Libraries.*
Texas State Library and Archives Commission. Revised edition of *The
CREW Manual* by Joseph Segal. http://www.tsl.state.tx.us/ld/pubs/
crew/.

> Step-by-step method for weeding using the CREW method
> (Continuous Review, Evaluation, and Weeding) and MUSTIE.
> Provides guidelines and rationale for a comprehensive sustained
> weeding program.

Buckingham, B. J. 1994. *Weeding the Library Media Center Collections.*
http://www.iema-ia.org/IEMA209.html.

> From the Iowa Department of Education, sound advice for weeding.

Johnson, D. 2003. *Weed.* http://www.doug-johnson.com/dougwri/weed.html.

> Humorous first-person account of weeding a collection based on sound principles.

Johnson, D. 2001. *Weeding the Neglected Collection.* http://www.doug-johnson.com/dougwri/weeding.html (update of a *School Library Journal* article from November 1990).

> First-year library media specialist recognizes the need to weed and does it! The results and advice.

Klopfer, K. *Weed It! For an Attractive and Useful Collection.* http://www.wmrls.org/services/colldev/weed_it.html.

> General weeding advice, including dealing with staff and the public.

Lamb, A. *Collection Maintenance and Weeding.* http://eduscapes.com/sms/weeding.html.

> Overview of the weeding process with links to resources and more information.

Lindsay, K. *An Ode to a Teacher-Librarian: Making Your Poetry Section Come Alive.* http://www.schoollibraries.ca/articles/30.aspx.

> Although the title focuses on poetry, the article suggests starting your weeding with the poetry section, gives a rationale for doing so, and provides a good overview of weeding in general.

Livingston, S. 1997. *Weeding Library Media Center Collections.* http://www.pld.fayette.k12.ky.us/lms/weed.htm.

> Words of wisdom and practical advice on weeding from a school library media specialist in Jefferson County, Kentucky.

Maryland State Department of Education. *"Weeding": Reassessment of Library Media Collections* [Microsoft Word document]. http://www.infohio.org/Documents/UC/WeedingGuidelinesMaryland.doc.

> Rationale and criteria for weeding school library media collections.

School Board of Alachua County (FL). *Guidelines for Weeding Library Materials.* http://www.sbac.edu/%7Emedia/guid_weeding.html.

> Seven general guidelines for weeding school library media collections.

School District of Philadelphia. 2001. *School Library Handbook: Weeding Library Materials.* http://www.libraries.phila.k12.pa.us/handbook/handbook-weeding.html.

> Reasons for weeding, criteria, and procedures from a large metropolitan school district.

Theis, A., and V. Nesting. 2005. *Weeding the Fiction Collection: Should I Dump Peyton Place?* http://www.overbooked.org/ra/weeding.html.

> A collection of resources for evaluating fiction materials, especially in the public library.

Weeding in Libraries: A Partial Index to What's Out There. http://www
.havana.lib.il.us/library/weeding.html.

> Links to weeding tools and information. Includes a bibliography of
> articles and resources.

Related

Baltimore County (MD) Public Schools. *Selection Criteria for School
Library Media Center Collections.* http://www.bcps.org/offices/lis/
office/admin/selection.html.

> Includes weeding, inventory, and reconsideration policies and
> procedures.

McKenzie, J. 2000. *The New Vertical File: Delivering Great Images and
Data to the Desktop.* http://www.fno.org/oct00/vertical.html.

GENERAL WEEDING CRITERIA BY DEWEY CLASSIFICATION

| Dewey Class | Subject | Retention | | Notes | Weeding Topics (by Dewey) Included in This Book |
		Ideal (years)	Maximum (years)		
000s	Generalities	5	10	Replace encyclopedias every 3–5 years; do not circulate older sets beyond 7–8 years; evaluate by use, especially curiosities and wonders	001.9—Curiosities and Wonders
001s–010s	Computers	3	5	A rapidly changing area; materials are not very useful after 3 years, especially for software; retain older programs and models according to demand; consider purchasing paperbacks	004—Computer Science
020s	Library Science	5	10	Keep classics; toss anything that doesn't conform to current practice and standards; watch for dated pictures and stereotypes	025—Libraries and Librarians
100s	Philosophy, Psychology	5	10	Self-help books become dated very quickly; classic titles may have newer editions; watch for dated concepts and pictures; evaluate by use	170—Moral Education
200s	Religion, Mythology	10	15	Evaluate by use and circulation; be sure something current is in the collection representing all major religions; myths may have newer editions	200—Religion
300s	Social Science	5	10	A very broad area; some controversial topics in this area; be sure the collection is balanced and current	301—Black History 302—Conflict Management 305.4—Women's Issues
310s	Almanacs, Yearbooks	2	5	Replace annually; use newest edition for reference and recent editions for circulating collection	

| Dewey Class | Subject | Retention | | Notes | Weeding Topics (by Dewey) Included in This Book |
		Ideal (years)	Maximum (years)		
320s–330s	Politics, Economics	5	10	Watch for out-of-date contacts; economics area is changing quickly —keep current	321.8—Democracy 322—Terrorism 323—Civil Rights 324—Presidential Elections 325—Immigration 330—Personal Finance 331—Careers 332—The Stock Market
340s–350s	Law, Government	5	10	Evaluate by use and relevance to curriculum	
360s	Social Services	5	10	Criminology is a hot topic; be sure current practice is reflected	360—Drug and Alcohol Education 362.4—Disabilities 363.2—Forensic Science
370s	Education	5	10	Many titles in your professional collection will be found here; titles should reflect current practice; make sure you have titles on test-taking and assessment; keep college guides until replacements arrive, especially for local schools; build in areas of particular interest to your school's philosophy and practice	370—Education
380s	Commerce, Communication, Careers	5	10	Watch for stereotypes, gender bias, and dated images; be sure career materials include applications of computers and modern technologies; communication should include wireless and mobile applications	380—Transportation
390s	Customs, Etiquette	10	15	Toss dated dating books; review etiquette materials—the rules have changed; weed by use and condition	392—Dating and Courtship
394s	General Customs	10	15	Holiday books are popular; save until you can update but toss those in poor condition	394—Holidays
398s	Folklore	10	20	Evaluate use and condition; replace well-used materials with newer editions	398—Folktales

Dewey Class	Subject	Retention		Notes	Weeding Topics (by Dewey) Included in This Book
		Ideal (years)	Maxi-mum (years)		
400s	Languages, Dictionaries	5	10	Look for technology-related words (DVD, CD, MP3, podcast, weblog) and slang that has come into common usage; check foreign-language and English as a second language materials for condition if popular and well used; picture dictionaries are good for ESL students if illustrations are not dated; grammar doesn't change much, but examples and illustra-tions can date materials	400—Languages (420—English)
500s	Natural Sciences, Mathematics	3	5	Keep classic works like Darwin and Rachel Carson, but keep up with new discoveries and theories; science fairs demand more frequent updating	507.8—Science Experiments
510s	Mathematics	8–10	15	Math doesn't change very much; weed by use and condition; keep historical and classic	510—Mathematics
520s	Astronomy	5	10	Recent discoveries in planets and the solar system should be reflected in materials	520—Space and Astronomy
530s–550s	Physics, Chemistry, Earth Science	5	10	Weather and climate books should include the use of technology; discard chemistry books that do not have the correct number of ele-ments; geology books should include information on continental drift and plate tectonics; guides to rocks, gems, minerals, etc., may be kept longer if in good condition	551.2—Earthquakes and Volcanoes 551.6—Weather
560s	Paleontology	5	10	Be sure materials describe five king-doms; dinosaur books should reflect current theories, including feathered creatures and upright tails; current nomenclature	567.9—Dinosaurs
570s	Biology	3	5	Keep taxonomies; microbiology is a hot topic; update information on viruses, bacteria	576—Genetic Engineering 576.8—Evolution 577—Ecology
580s–590s	Botany, Zoology	5	10	Not much changes here; weed by condition and use; keep up with current list of endangered species	597—Reptiles and Amphibians

| Dewey Class | Subject | Retention | | Notes | Weeding Topics (by Dewey) Included in This Book |
		Ideal (years)	Maximum (years)		
600s–620s	Applied Science, Technology, Medicine, Mechanics, Engineering	3	5	Toss any older materials that may be misleading; science fair materials and topics should be current; diet and exercise titles may be retained longer; be sure materials on sexually transmitted diseases include current information on AIDS; include materials on growing fields of nanotechnology and microbiology; aviation titles should include international space station, space shuttle status	600s—Vocational Trades 613.2—Nutrition 613.7—Physical Fitness 613.85—Tobacco Education 614.5—AIDS 616—Diseases 629.1—Aviation History
630s	Agriculture, Farm, Gardens, Domestic Animals	5	15	Be sure materials reflect new trends in farming and gardening; pet materials are always popular, but get rid of those that don't leave the shelves; update more often if you serve agricultural or farming communities; toss anything that promotes harmful or banned pesticides like DDT	
640s	Family Studies, Cookbooks, Home Economics	3	10	Cookbooks should reflect the latest nutrition and medical information; current cooking trends should be reflected: ethnic, low-fat, low-carb; materials should reflect safe food-handling techniques; watch for sexist images and stereotyping in family studies and home economics materials; fashion goes out of fashion quickly—toss after 3 years; babysitting and parenting materials should reflect current research and practice	641.5—Cooking
650s	Business Management, Public Relations	3	5	Weed interviewing and résumé writing frequently; typing is out—people keyboard now; make sure uses of technology in business reflect current practice in text and images; monitors have flat screens; handhelds, laptops, and tablets are commonplace; watch out for stereotyping in images	
660s–690s	Chemical Engineering, Manufacturing, Building Construction	5	10	Keep materials on collectibles; make sure the use of computers is included; be aware of modern materials and techniques	

| Dewey Class | Subject | Retention | | Notes | Weeding Topics (by Dewey) Included in This Book |
		Ideal (years)	Maximum (years)		
700s	Art, Music, Sports	5	10	Art and music: get new editions of well-used titles; keep histories of art and music if in good condition; keep sports classics, but newer editions may be available	
740s	Crafts	5	10	Crafts have life cycles: keep one copy of a good book on fading fads—macramé, decoupage, tie-dye, etc.; add today's hobbies and crafts; materials for crafts and hobbies have changed dramatically; retain basic technique books	740—Hobbies and Crafts 741—Drawing and Cartooning
770s	Photography	3	10	Digital photography is popular and rapidly changing—keep up; toss items with dated equipment and techniques; keep basic darkroom titles for hobbyists	770—Photography
780s	Music	5	10	Be sure you have something on rap, country, and electronic music; keep well-used histories, but replace if worn or damaged	780—Music
790s	Sports	5	10	Watch out for teams that have moved: Boston-Milwaukee-Atlanta Braves, etc.; be mindful of expansion teams in all sports; replace well-used titles with newer editions; be aware that rules in sports do change; reflect growing interest in extreme sports	792.8—Dance 796—Sports 796.357—Baseball 796.48—Olympic Games
800s	Literature	5	15	Keep basics and classics; check indexes before discarding poetry; check for dust, must, mold, mildew—and especially use	808—Poetry 808.7—Wit and Humor 822.3—Shakespeare
900s	History	5	10	Check demand, accuracy, condition; monitor information on areas of change: countries of the former Soviet Union, Afghanistan, Africa, the Middle East, and Eastern Europe; be ruthless	
910s	Travel, Geography	2	5	Outdated travel guides are useless; replace on rotating basis, every 2 or 3 years	910—Geography

Dewey Class	Subject	Retention Ideal (years)	Maximum (years)	Notes	Weeding Topics (by Dewey) Included in This Book
920s	Biography	5	10	Keep biographies that support the curriculum (artists, presidents, inventors, world leaders, etc.) and update those that kids enjoy (rock stars, musicians, athletes)	920—Biography
930s–990s	History	10	15	World War II continues to be popular, but you should have something on Spanish American War, Korean War, Vietnam, and the Gulf conflicts; examine all materials carefully for bias; accuracy of facts and fairness of interpretation are key; maintain primary source materials if in good condition or replace; immigrant groups should include most recent, not just European; eliminate any stereotypes in Native American materials (or any other group); remember 1960s, 1970s, and 1980s are ancient history to students— maintain some accurate representative works; maintain local history and items that get heavy use in classroom assignments	940—Europe 940.53—The Holocaust 940.53—World War II 947—Russia 959.7—Vietnam 960—Africa 970.004—Native Americans 971–972—Canada and Mexico 972.91—Cuba 973—U.S. Presidents 973.7—The Civil War 973.93—September 11
Fiction/ Easy/Story Collections		5	15	Toss duplicate copies of items with low circulation; watch for outdated topics, topics appropriate for reading level; keep high demand, award winners, popular authors' works; condition and use will determine keeping or tossing; replace old favorites with new editions; quality picture books remain popular; YA titles should appeal to YAs	FIC—Fiction SC—Short Stories
Reference		3	10	These materials should include the most current information; toss or return to circulation anything over 10 years old; update well-used with newer editions; some areas age quickly and will need to be replaced every year or two, others will last for 10 years or more; anything over 20 years old needs to go	REF—Reference

Dewey Class	Subject	Retention		Notes	Weeding Topics (by Dewey) Included in This Book
		Ideal (years)	**Maxi-mum** *(years)*		
AV		varies		Older formats should be removed from shelves: filmstrips, sound film-strips, 8 mm and 16 mm films, film loops, 5.25- and 3.5-inch diskettes; videotapes have limited life	
Vertical File		varies		With the World Wide Web as a source, vertical files are as obsolete as many AV formats; images, docu-ments, and artifacts that support the curriculum are available in digital format; spend your time locat-ing and organizing those for best use; a small local file may be useful, however, for topics of local interest; weed thoroughly and annually if you have a vertical file	
Periodicals		varies		Keep for a short time if you get hard copy; most resources students need are available online; weigh the cost of storage, binding, maintenance of hard copy against cost of CD-ROM or online resources	
Gift Materials		by classification		Must meet the same criteria as other materials; remove those that don't circulate; refuse or discard any that are biased, inaccurate, misleading, worn, or duplicates	

ALPHABETICAL INDEX

INDEX BY DEWEY CLASSIFICATION

Donna Baumbach has spent most of her career working with and for school library media specialists and supporting teachers' use of instructional technology. She is a professor of Instructional Technology/ Educational Media at the University of Central Florida in Orlando and Director of the Florida SUNLINK Project, the state K–12 public school union catalog of library media resources. Baumbach was named Instructional Technology Leader of the Year by the International Society for Technology in Education and was the recipient of the University of Central Florida's Presidential Award. She was the primary researcher for the Florida study of library media programs, *Making the Grade*, and is a frequent speaker at library and technology conferences. Baumbach earned her doctorate in Instructional Systems Technology from Indiana University with minors and extensive coursework in both library and information science and telecommunications.

Linda Miller is the Associate Director of the Florida SUNLINK Project, the state K–12 public school union catalog of library media resources. Miller earned her master's degree in Library Science from the University of Michigan. Miller is a former editor of *Florida Media Quarterly* and compiles the monthly electronic newsletter for SUNLINK schools. She has held positions as a school library media specialist (elementary, middle, and high school), academic cataloger, academic and public reference librarian, and graduate-level adjunct instructor of cataloging.